The Samuel Sessions

*A Collection of Sessions, Essays, Transcripts and Revelations
for achieving Higher Spiritual Guidance,
understanding the nature of the Multi-Dimensional Universe
and discovering your Essence Path*

E. M. Nicolay and H. L. Jang

An EssencePath Handbook to Higher Levels of Spiritual Guidance

Forethought Publishing

Copyright © 2019 by E. M. Nicolay and H.L. Jang
Cover & Text Design by FTC Group

All rights reserved. This book may not be reproduced in whole or in part without written permission from the publisher, except by a reviewer who may quote brief passages in a review; nor may any part of this book be reproduced, stored in a retrieval system, or transmitted in any form or by any means electronic, mechanical, photocopying, recording, or other, without written permission form the publisher.

Forethought Publishing
1900 John F. Kennedy Blvd., Suite 323, Philadelphia PA 19103

Contents

Chapter 1	**The Multi Dimensional Universe**	
	● The Multi Dimensional Universe	2
	● Collapse of the Current Time Paradigm	9
	● You Are a Multi-Dimensional Being	13
	● Dreams, The Astral Planes & The Afterlife	18
Chapter 2	**Planet Earth**	
	❋ Earth Day	22
	❋ Oil Spills	23
	❋ The Earth's Chakra System & "Un-Natural" Natural Disasters	27
Chapter 3	***2012***	
	❋ 2012	34
	❋ The Significance of 12-21-12	39
Chapter 4	**Finding Your Own Truth**	
	▩ Truth & The Integrity of Your Soul	48
	▩ When Seeking Truth...	62
	▩ Expressing Your Energy in Uncertain Times	69
	▩ The Guidance You Attract	72
	▩ Unmasking Your Truth	75
	▩ When Adversity Seems Relentless	79
	▩ Privacy, please! How Truth & Privacy are Lessons in Respectfulness	91
Chapter 5	**The Creation of Physical Reality**	
	☙ Conscious Intention	104
	☙ The Power of Creation	110

Contents

	❦ The Expression of Your Will	113
	❦ The Power of Words, Thought Control and the Altering of Physical Reality	120
	❦ Group Intention and Reality Manifestation	128

Chapter 6   **Earthly Existence - On Health, Relationships and Money**
- Becoming Whole   136
- The Question of Relationship   142
- The Money Paradigm   149

Chapter 7   **Fear, Faith and Physical Reality Creation**
- Finding Your Way to Neutral   156
- Where there is Light, Darkness cannot exist   170

Chapter 8   **Symbols and Symbolism**
- The Language of Symbols   180
- The Meaning of 11:11   191

Related Books in the Essence Path Series   196

The Essence Path Series - Book Four:
"Timeline Collapse & Universal Ascension: The Future of Third Dimensional Earth and Fifth Dimensional Terra"
A riveting look at world events seen on the future timeline of Earth from now until 2569, and an exploration of the Ascension of Human Angelics to Earth's Fifth Dimensional Counterpart, Terra.

The Essence Path Series - Book Three:
"The System Lords and the Twelve Dimensions: New Revelations Concerning the Dimensional Shift of 2012-2250 and the Evolution of Human Angelics"
An analysis of coming Earth changes, the reasons an intensification of energy is

Contents

coming from the Galactic core and altering our Solar System at this time, the collapse of our dimensional time line, the evolution of our DNA, the structure of the multi-dimensional universe and how the vibrational quality of our beliefs, emotions, thoughts and choices combine to raise our cellular resonance.

The Essence Path Series - Book Two:
"Fear, Faith and Physical Reality"
Building on the themes begun in Book One, "Fear, Faith and Physical Reality" provides a more complete analysis of coming vibrational changes, a description of the coming emergence of 4th dimension attributes within the 3rd dimension, the nature of universal dimensional overlap, the polarity of belief, emotion and thought and your relationship to the manifestation of your personal reality.

The Essence Path Series - Book One:
"Discovering Your Essencepath Path and Other Quintessential Phenomena"
An exploration of the nature of our causal reality and its relationship to thought, feeling and the fabric of life, the multi-dimensional nature of your Soul and its journey, the truth about higher guidance in the Third Dimensional realm, the real nature of alien visitation, the world altering energetic changes we are facing, how dreams and the astral state contribute to the fabric of our reality, and the reasons why increasing your energetic vibration through the pursuit of higher consciousness is particularly important during this monumental Ascension time period.

Chapter 1
The Multi Dimensional Universe

The Multi Dimensional Universe

The Universe is multi-dimensional and consists of twelve what we shall call "Universal Dimensions". Each Universal Dimension vibrates at a specific frequency, and what is visible in one dimension may not be visible in another dimension. This is particularly true in that higher dimensional levels, in general, can see and experience lower dimensional levels, but lower levels have great difficulty "seeing" higher dimensional realms. Thus you personally might exist at a certain level of the Third Universal Dimension and be aware of the existence of Second and First dimensional beings, such as the plant and mineral kingdom, where despite the fact that you cannot actually communicate or participate directly in their existence, you nevertheless have the ability to interact and, to an extent, have dominion over their environment. In much the same manner, you yourselves may not have direct awareness of Fifth or Sixth Dimensional beings living their lives alongside you, though we assure you that they are generally as aware of you as you are of the giant redwood or the boulder outside your window.

There are nine Universal Dimensional levels that we will call the dimensions of experience, and there are three additional levels: the Tenth, Eleventh and Twelfth Universal Dimensions that begin the realms of completion, the realm of All That Is or the Creator God Force, if you will. In truth, we must add that the Creator itself extends beyond the Twelfth Universal Dimension and is present at the Tenth, Eleventh and Twelfth Universal Dimensional levels, the places of highest light, wisdom and enlightenment. It is within these realms that those who have evolved to this point begin the process of reintegration with All That Is at levels and understanding that are beyond most beings in the lower universal levels can fathom.

These three Universal Dimensions (the Tenth, Eleventh and Twelfth) are rare dimensions of the highest nature and order. While these dimensions are indeed independent of each other, they are also unified and could be said to serve as the basis for what you know as the "Trinity" symbolism. They are truly the dimensions most closely associated with what you would term God or All That Is, individuated just as the Trinity consciousness is in Christian and other religions, yet unified as the ultimate beginning of integration into All That Is. While it is natural for the entities within the Third Dimensional realm, as well as the Second and First Dimensions, to see everything with a higher or lower hierarchy, this is not necessarily the case with these three highest dimensions. The Tenth or the Eleventh Dimension is not necessarily higher or lower than the Twelfth Dimension. However the Tenth, Eleventh and Twelfth Dimensions are unified in God-likeness and All That Is, Nirvana, if you wish to term it, or even perhaps the ultimate experience of Heaven in the western way of thinking. These are, in fact, the highest Universal Dimensions obtainable by evolving beings and consciousness prior to entry into the realms of pure spirit where only the God Force exists.

The Universal Dimensions themselves are physically separated in various parts of the Universe. Each Universal Dimension can only be seen by Souls who have reached the maturing stage or vibrational frequency of that Universal Dimension. For example, Third Universal Dimensional Beings would not be able to see the Fifth or Sixth Universal Dimensions until they complete the learning process of the Third Universal Dimension and reach the vibrational frequency of those Universal Dimensions. Fifth or Sixth Universal Dimensions are thus seen as the faraway galaxies and Solar Systems only glimpsed in the night sky by those incarnated within the Third Universal Dimension.

Since time and space are not structured as you think and, indeed, are unified wave and frequency structures, though enormous distance appears to be the case from a Third Dimensional perspective, the reality is these faraway galaxies and Solar Systems are actually quite close and, in some cases, even overlap. A Sixth Universal Dimensional Being, for example, would be able to witness the Third Universal Dimension as much closer to and perhaps even unified in some manner with their own dimension, just as you witness and might interact with a tree or mountain in your reality, though it is not likely you would participate in the "being-ness" of trees or mountains. Every Soul then progresses through each of these Universal Dimensions, and it must be noted that there is not necessarily a specific order followed in terms of progression. However, there is, in general, a format that is followed by most whereby there is a natural progression that corresponds to each entity's vibrational frequency, usually achieved by the natural evolution and elevation of consciousness. This evolution, which applies to each Soul, each Being, all Solar Systems, all Galaxies and even the Universe at large, is known as Ascension.

Now there are dimensional forays within each Universal Dimension. Each Universal Dimension is further subdivided into twelve closely related sub-dimensional levels that overlap within the Universal Dimension. Thus, if you are hearing or reading this, you are living life currently at the third sub-dimensional level of the Third Universal Dimension. To be sure, there are vast properties and similarities that the Universal Dimensions share with the sub-dimensional levels related to them. When you, physical beings in the third sub-level of the Third Universal Dimension, communicate with those who have passed on from your physical reality, you are in fact communicating with those who now exist in a reality closely related to the fourth or fifth sub-dimensional reality of your Third Universal Dimension, and these Souls cycle to higher sublevels, or astral planes as they are commonly known, of the Third Universal Dimension, as they await reintegration with their Soul and related life reincarnations.

As we have explained, for the most part they can "see" you, but there is still much debate from your side as to whether or not they even exist. This is one of the great ironies of universal interplay.

Compounds, substances, minerals and mountains are typically First Dimensional Beings. They evolve to become plant life and animal life that are generally Second Dimensional Beings. Other First and Second Dimensional Beings are found in the Devic Kingdom--the fairies, elves and trolls of your mythology are an expression of these energies closely linked to the life experience of the plant and Second Dimensional kingdom. For the most part, first and second dimensional beings do not have individualized Souls but have what we would call hive Souls, where they are part of a Soul group such as all "plant-ness," all "cow-ness," all "rock-ness," and, ultimately, as they evolve higher, they offshoot and become individualized Souls that Ascend to the next level of sentient incarnation. It is quite possible that any one among you may have had their first origins, prior to becoming an individualized Soul, experiencing life as part of "rock-ness" or with origins from any of the other Devic or other lower dimensional kingdoms. The possibilities are, literally, endless.

First and Second Dimensional beings co-exist with beings, such as you, positioned at the third sub-level dimension of Third Universal Dimension. Humans can see certain aspects of First and Second Dimensional Being properties, but, to be clear, there are also certain aspects that humans cannot, or prefer not, to see.

For example, you can see the mountain, but you cannot see the mountain evolving or see it energetically, with a purpose, a mission, a desire, a feeling and a structure. Similarly, you can not see these beings after their existence, or incarnation, is complete. Typically, you do not picture mountains as separate and distinct but see them as a group. Similarly, you see a field of flowers, but you do not see the energetic waves of expression around them − the "fairies," anthropomorphized representations of the flowers' etheric body. As we said before, most humans incarnated at the third sublevel of the Third Universal Dimension today have in fact evolved, over eons of chronological time, from the first and second Universal Dimensions.

Approximately every 26,000 years, the Souls within a Universal Dimension are able to transcend to higher levels of consciousness within their own Universal Dimension. Thus, as an example, a Soul might no longer need to incarnate at the third sublevel of the Third Universal Dimension and might choose instead to remain in higher sublevels, such as the fifth, seventh or even eighth sublevel of the Third Universal Dimension. Some might view these higher sublevels of the Third Universal Dimension as different areas of the Astral Plane, the "Paradise" or Heaven known to your mythology and folk stories, or even as parallel worlds.

Every 250,000 years, due to the energetic nature of the Universe and the "waves" that come from the Creator--All that Is--this same process of transcendence is available not only within the sublevels of a Universal Dimension, but also for the Universal Dimension as a whole. And it follows that this then applies to the Ascension of each Soul from one Universal Dimension to the next Universal Dimension.

In a free-will Universe such as this one, each Soul has the ability to choose not to Ascend and, some may in fact choose to remain within the Third Universal Dimension. At the time of Ascension then, the Third Universal Dimension into which those Souls will continue to incarnate will actually be the former Second Universal Dimension, which has Ascended to take its place as the Third Universal Dimension via the Ascension process. For those Souls that choose Ascension, they will incarnate on an Earth that was once within the Third Universal Dimension but that now is in the Fourth or Fifth Universal Dimension, having transcended or Ascended.

To complicate the matter further, Ascension is not necessarily linear in fashion. It is possible therefore, for entities that have reached certain levels of consciousness upon Ascension to transcend and ascend in a non-linear manner. The multi-dimensional nature of the Universe permits those entities that have attained a certain level of consciousness to go directly from say Third Universal Dimension incarnations to Fifth or even Sixth Universal Dimension incarnations depending on the level of consciousness their prior incarnations have allowed them to achieve.

Currently your realm is at a miraculous turning point, for not only does the current age represent the 26,000 year point at which Souls are able to automatically graduate from a particular sub-dimensional level, but also you are at a significant point in universal history, since this time period also relates to the approximately 250 million-year process that enables your entire Solar System and the Galaxy, as a whole, to Ascend to the next Universal Dimension vibration. This is extraordinary, for the period you are now in represents the manner in which Solar Systems and Galaxies evolve, and universal Ascension, meaning a growth of resonance and consciousness that allows every Soul, every Being and entire realms of existence to transcend to a higher consciousness and dimensional level of consciousness within the multi-dimensional Universe, is currently at hand. This, then, is the true meaning of "Ascension."

Collapse of the Current Time Paradigm

You live in miraculous times and it is not by accident that you have chosen to be present in this particular time period. For as we have said in the past, it should be known that what distinguishes a dimension, what actually creates dimensional flow is the wavelength of time or rather perhaps more precisely said, the wavelength of time forms the dimension in which you find yourself.

Now truly, someone would be hard pressed to say that they have not noticed lately that time is speeding up. What was a month is now a week. What was a day is now an hour. This is not by accident. For in the Ascension process, the evolutionary process in which you are now taking part, the current time wave that you are in, the time line that actually creates the dimension of which you are a part, is in fact collapsing. Perhaps this is too frightening a word for you so allow us to explain by first stating that we are not discussing here the actual demise of time, although one could conclude that is truly. the case.

However, what is more precise is to say that time, the frequency of the time wave that delineates and denotes your current dimension is evolving and expanding. But before this takes place, there is a flattening of that same time wave that takes place. So if you were to see this as a wave, as we suggest and as any frequency is, and you were to see your entire dimension as a spiraling wave related to the experience of time, you would begin to see that the waves are shortening and becoming smaller as they pass you. As they become shorter, things speed up, with the eventuality that ultimately the time wave you know will quite literally as well as figuratively "flat line."

This does not mean the death or end of your dimension as it might suggest. However, it is the evolution of your dimension into the next time wave and subsequently, the next dimensional vibration. What is important about this is that different time waves and frequencies also provide different perceptive abilities, usually energetic in nature, within a particular dimension. Your current time line parameters included the fact that you are not necessarily able to understand or perceive higher energetic dimensional and physical properties. But as you move into the next time wave, after you have reached the point the current spiral time wave is flattened, the wave begins again on the opposite side. And as that wave begins on the other side, so also do you begin again.

If you have chosen to be in this particular incarnation at this particular time, it is because you know that being in a lifetime during this period is equivalent in terms of energetic intensity, as it relates to the amount that is experienced and the growth possible for your Soul, to the potential learning and growth allotted over the course of perhaps twenty–five (25) lifetimes of what you would typically experience with the normal cascade of time in a usual time wave and dimension. It is for this reason that such extreme intensity and urgency is being felt on Earth and in your lives. For the Earth is indeed birthing itself into the coming new timeline and as a result is experiencing coming dimensional transformation. This momentary rev in time caused by the flattening of the timeline will in fact ensure that each of you who are connected to this dimensional sphere will, together with the Earth, evolve and Ascend into the next dimensional time sequence.

For most, your future incarnations will take place within a new energetic frequency, and this new level will provide a myriad of new opportunities for growth available to all those evolving and incarnating with Earth. This is the heritage and the meaning of Ascension as the evolutionary tool of the Universe, and you are assured of this if you actively choose to Ascend at this time. If you are hearing these words and are a part of this group, though you are not exclusive or a member of any elite, you can in fact be said to have obtained the consciousness necessary to hear this message and this in turn signals that you have done the work necessary to assist your Soul in Ascending and evolving its incarnations to the next level of existence.

Do not fear that those with whom you are also currently incarnated, those with whom you have karma or those you love, will not accompany you. For in truth, the great majority of those incarnated on Earth at this time will take part in this shift of consciousness and coming Ascension. You merely represent those Souls who have understood what is happening first, and as leaders in this you hold greater responsibility in terms of your choices and the manifestation of your reality, particularly in providing others with the Truth and Light energy that you have discovered.

Many will sense that something is different and many among them will fear and think something in their life is wrong. It is this impetus that inspires you to go seek Truth at this time, and it is this that leads many to want to shout to the powers in charge of the cultural and political structures of your realm that enough is enough. This is because as you evolve, it is no longer possible to live in a world of distrust, fear and deceit, just as in the new dimensional zone you are entering, it is not possible for an evolved immune system to exist within the toxic environment that has been created in the former (your current) timeline. So what you witness is an innate desire to change the world so that it is a world that is more compatible with what is happening to you and who you are becoming energetically. This will continue to intensify through the coming year and will be present well beyond.

While the evolution will not be completed at the mystical pinnacle we described as the 2012 time frame much touted by those who would have you fear this to be the end of the world, the fact is that 2012 does indeed represent a critical high point in this transformation and evolution. It is at this marker that you have crossed the threshold of the new time line we are discussing, and it can be seen as a new period that you have entered.

While you will continue to rise each morning as you have and though there will continue to be turmoil in your world, you will find after 2012 that for the most part, particularly if you are aligned with your own truth and with this information in a conscious way, you have in fact turned the corner. While others around you may continue to struggle, for each must proceed into the new time wave and dimension at their own pace, you, the fortunate ones who have raised their consciousness and frequency to meet the demand of the new time wave, will see that the devastation happening around you might be problematic and cause fear for others but it is in fact unable to touch or reach you.

This is because having aligned yourself with your Truth you have Ascended into a higher frequency and are moving together with, instead of against, the new vibration taking hold on Earth. Think of yourselves as trendsetters, who through your consciousness, your commitment to a higher, personal Truth, your adherence to the higher, lighter frequencies of light and your understanding that what is happening is the Ascension process are first to be drawn into a new body, in a new world, a new time wave and a new multi-dimensional existence.

As you go about your lives from here on out, expect others to instinctively seek you out or emulate you as the evolutionary trendsetters that you are. Then when you least expect it, there will come a time at some point over the course of the coming century when everyone and everything within your realm will reach unity within Ascension and you will move together into a brave new beginning.

You Are a Multi Dimensional Being

Be aware that you are principally spiritual beings having a physical experience. As such, you are multi-dimensional in nature, and the being you really are resides simultaneously in numerous dimensional frequencies or vibrations. It is unfortunate that because of your physical life focus and the subsequent necessity of physical limitation, you forget that your true origination is multi-dimensional in nature. However, because of the energy that is coming into the world at this time, you are once again able to sense, to realize and to discern the fact that you are in truth an extension of a spiritual being that has simultaneous projections of itself in many other universal realities.

We have described in the past the nature of overlap in the dimensional structure of the Universe, and we have explained already that there are essentially what we have termed twelve Universal Dimensions. You, that is, the life you are currently experiencing, exist in the Third Universal Dimension and there are sub levels to the Universal Dimensions through which beings like yourself evolve and advance. What is perhaps confusing to you is the fact that you believe that one dimension is here and another is there, one is over to the left and one is light years away from where you currently find yourself. But this is not the case. Dimensional overlap is intrinsic in universal structure, and Universal Dimensions are much closer than you ever imagined. In effect, each Universal Dimension overlaps the other, and there is considerable sharing, both energetically and even in terms of actual substance, between them.

This means that if you are incarnated in the third sub level of the Third Universal Dimension on what you know as Earth, you are in fact living within an energetic and, in some cases, real overlapping of first and Second Dimensional density. Although not "seen" in the way you may know, these dimensional values are none the less all around you, and one could even state that every time you look at a mountain range you are in fact witnessing a Second Dimensional entity. Every time you see a cloud, you behold the passing of a First Dimensional entity. And if you are able to grasp this truth, then why would you not believe as well that a Fourth or Fifth or even Sixth Dimensional existence is present side by side with you, overlapping and sometimes encompassing where you currently are.

Because you are beings realizing physical lifetimes in the Solar System that contains Earth, it is also this area where your Soul has essentially decided to incarnate again and again through, for the most part, the order of the twelve Universal Dimension cycles. While this is a general statement, and varies with each Soul, for the most part this means that when your Soul Ascends to incarnations in the Fifth, Sixth, Seventh or Eighth Dimensions, and beyond, you will not find yourself incarnated in some far flung reaches of a Universe with which you are not familiar. Instead, you will find yourself contained within your own area, albeit a vast one, and that is an area with which you have considerable expertise and accompanying knowledge.

Thus, when you are ready to Ascend and begin incarnations in the Fifth Universal Dimension, which, if your Soul origination is Human Angelic as we have explained, is your rightful destiny, you will in fact be incarnating in roughly the same area of space in which you currently find yourself. However, the physical attributes you perceive, due principally to the physical properties of universal structure, will seem familiar but never the less will be quite different for you. Because of this, a Fifth Dimensional Earth, known as Terra, is far different structurally than the Third Dimensional Earth you recognize and know well even though it occupies the same space, albeit at a different vibrational frequency.

As you evolve through universal structure in the process known as

Ascension, you will become experts in all things related to your quadrant of the Universe. You will grow experience, in opportunity and in wisdom based on new things that you create and develop that are founded on the expanding dimensional attributes you find along the way as you grow. But you will not, as you may think, find yourself in some foreign or far-flung Galaxy that is not native to your Soul. You will find yourself ultimately on an Earth that is higher dimensionally in nature, with the changes inherent in higher dimensional validity, but retaining a rather close proximity to your current positioning in terms of actual location and the space into which you currently project your reality. Where there is a Second Dimensional mountain range on Third Dimensional Earth, on Fifth Dimensional Terra there may be an ocean. Where there is a civilization in the Third Universal DImension, in Fifth Dimensional reality there may be a field of poppies. Whatever the case, do not be fooled for you have not left the location you know so well, you have simply changed your attunement and raised your oscillation to the point of seeing what you were not able to see when your consciousness resided at a different vibrational frequency.

More importantly as you go, become familiar with the energetic exchange that has been described in many ways, but is perhaps best understood as karma. We take karma to simply mean the dispelling and balancing of energy, and what you may not realize is that this balancing of energy is also a vital component of a multi-dimensional Universe where expansion is transcendent. Currently, you perhaps realize that you have numerous lifetimes situated in different time folds within the Third Universal Dimension. What you perhaps do not realize is that what you are creating and doing here does not dissipate but evolves and transcends in a never ending progression to higher and yet higher dimensional values.

In a multi-dimensional system, what you create energetically is not necessarily confined to your dimension, and for this reason what you, or your brethren, create in the Third Universal Dimension has bleed through and consequence on the energies that emerge in other dimensions. This is true within the sub levels of your Third Universal Dimension, say the Astral planes for example, where intense energetic occurrences in your world have an almost immediate and sometimes impactful effect on beings residing in other sub levels of the dimension that you may be unable to currently access completely. This is also true inter-dimensionally, where intense energetic happenings create a ripple effect and energetic waves are transferred from one Universal Dimension to another.

You do not, as you have perhaps been taught, leave behind any piece or part of you energetically. That which you created and navigated through in the Third Universal Dimension will also have a place in what you reap in the higher Universal Dimensions when and as you move forward. Granted, these experiences may be part of a greater Soul entity and may take on different forms, as they express themselves in new opportunities that are based on the physical structures inherent in higher dimension. And your way of dealing with these energies will also be afforded new opportunities for growth based on the higher-dimensional personal attributes you obtain, expanded sensibilities that give you new ways of analyzing the issues so you may invent new ways to experiment with and balance your creations.

But do understand here that the energies surrounding you will ultimately be the karma that not only lifts you to higher vibrational resonance but also actually serves as the basis for your opportunities for growth in the higher dimensions. Therefore, once again, be reminded that what you give, you shall receive in this lifetime, the lifetimes that are Third Dimensional in nature, and also in the lifetimes that you push into and experience in higher dimensional realms, albeit experienced and met with higher dimensional understanding and ability.

We leave you with the thought that much of what is being created now in your Third Dimensional world is a distraction, perhaps intentional, from your true purpose in existence. Do not be hypnotized or swayed from understanding that you are a multi-dimensional being focused on one of many singular experiences. You need only focus your attention on those areas that you wish to explore in order to have them materialized in your life. Hopefully, these same experiences will be of benefit to you in a higher dimensional realm, which, in every case and whether you believe it or not, will prove to be a journey as rewarding as the journey you have already experienced ascending through the first, the second and, now, the Third Universal Dimensions. We bring you much love and peace, and wish for you every success on your journey forward from Third Universal Dimension reality into Fifth Dimensional Ascension, which many of you have already begun.

Dreams, The Astral Planes & The Afterlife

Q: What happens when people pass on in terms of dimensions and energy? What really happens when you communicate with people who pass on? Where do they go? Are they still in the Third Dimension but in a different energy form? Or have they moved on to a different dimension all together?

Once again, this is a question that cannot be answered in simple terms. In general, those individuals who pass on from physical incarnation remain within a higher vibrational dimension related to the Third Universal Dimension and it could be said they have transferred to a dimensional reality that is closer to the Fourth Dimensional reality but is not actually Fourth Universal Dimensional in nature. In general, this is the level where entities await for their new incarnations in Third Dimensional reality. As the deceased pass, they reach a higher level of dimensional frequency, since they discard their dense physical bodies, where they remain until such time as they are unified back into the higher understanding that could be said to emanate from their Higher Self or Soul. This also entails understanding how the life incarnation they have just lived melds and works together with all the life times of the Soul. Finally, in conjunction with their Higher Self -- whom many see as God or a Guide of sorts -- they orchestrate the blending of their energy within a new incarnation once they have reviewed and, in some instances, relived events from the prior physical life time. In many ways, the dimensional reality where they initially find themselves is very much related to what you would term the dream state. It has also been known as the astral state. While they are not completely unified back into the energy of their Higher Self, they do have what we would call transference potential, and this is specifically the reason why many who have passed do in fact come and "visit" those still in physical incarnation while the latter is within the dream state or the dream reality.

We would add that in general these types of transference episodes (while dreaming) are not mere fantasies but actually, in most cases, are visitations from those they have known in life. When one accesses from the physical third dimensional sub level those who are in higher astral state, it is very similar to the manner in which many access higher guidance, and therefore seems to have an association for most with what is popularly know as angels or guides for there are similarities indeed.

While these kinds of communications are possible, we would add that in simple terms those who have passed from physical incarnation are rejoining the greater part of themselves in leaving the physical lifetime, but by no means do they disappear. Rather, the process is one of transferring energy back to where each of you is originally derived.

In other words, taking on physical existence is, in a certain sense, a diminished point of view that is obtained by the necessity of the Higher Self taking on a physical body. That same physical lifetime, when discarded, is not completely torn away but is taken off in a physical sense only. Then it is looked at, explored and ultimately integrated in an astral sense as time warrants and as each entity, in conjunction with their Higher Self, prefers.

This is the reason why we would suggest that if you were to take a look at the concept of visitations or "ghost" so to speak, we would say that it would be rare for you to find such entities wandering the earth more than two hundred, three hundred or perhaps four hundred of your Earth years at the most. This is because while each individual in astral transition will ultimately begin to understand what has happened (physical death) to them, in many cases those that you would term "ghosts," do not yet have this understanding. Until they become aware of the cessation of their physical beings, they wander around places that they recognize or had attachment to while in the physical body. Once they begin the process of moving through the Astral Plane and the higher Astral Planes to a point where they are no longer linked to physical reality, however, and have reached a point where there is less communication with the physical dimension, they progress to the point of return to their Soul and the potential of reaching new physical incarnation. We would add also that this is the reason why when loved ones have passed, they seem so close to you for a year or maybe two, and sometimes longer, but as time progresses in the physical realm, you notice that there is less sense of contact with them.

Most still within physical reality assume this means that they themselves have moved on in their physical lives to a point where they no longer are so closely connected with the pain caused by the loved one's departure. However, we would say that the loved one has actually moved on within the astral and higher astral dimension, and therefore ceased communication or contact with you in the dream state as they continue the process of their return to all knowing and their Higher Self – in other words, the unification with their Soul.

 ## Chapter 2
Planet Earth

Earth Day

We are pleased to meet again and are honored to be with you on a day that has become commonly known as Earth Day. Many would think that this is a newly found awareness — a concept that those within the Earth plane have evolved to only recently. However, to the contrary, we would say that this awareness, the understanding that those who treat the Earth with respect are in reality respecting selves, is a notion that is paramount and primal. In fact, it is a belief that is the foundation of the Earth realm and was prominent early in your current cycle of history. For if you look back within your own linear time line historically, you will find that in the Earth realm originally, all of the primal religions and all of the shamanic and related practices were identified with and based upon the sacredness of the Earth. This was forgotten over the course of your time, and ultimately respect of the Earth was substituted and projected outside of your own being onto an invisible regulating, external power. While this facilitated the growth of certain societal organizations that used a newly externalized force to cement the position and power of some for the so-called benefit of all, it caused a block and disintegration of the natural connection all physical beings that inhabited the realm have with the body of Earth itself.

Now during this miraculous time, you have begun once again to witness and find your connection to Earth. This is not by accident. Indeed, it is the first step to an evolution that allows each and every individual incarnated in the sphere to understand his or her connection with not only Earth but ultimately, with All That Is. It is the first step in understanding that you and the Earth are one, which you and every individual, every living being and every other living part of creation share commonality as you participate in this miraculous creation.

So it is a blessing that this sacred connection has in fact been not newly discovered, as many would believe, but re-discovered. For as we said, your understanding of the connection you have with Earth is the first step to understand the coming miraculous age -- an age where each of you will consciously re-discover a connection to how you co-create your reality within this realm. And in doing so, you evolve to the next level of wisdom as you find, once again, your place not only within the Earth sphere but within the Universal Dimensions of which you are so miraculously and expertly connected in endless multi-dimensional ways.

Oil Spills

Q: This question concerns the oil spill in the Gulf Coast. Does the ocean have the ability to heal itself? A body can sometimes heal itself with natural remedies. Is the ocean able to heal itself from what's going on with this terrible oil spill?

First of all, we must say that what is occurring is a tragedy beyond comparison. It is a tragedy beyond comparison because it is not at all a "natural" occurrence. To answer your question directly "Yes indeed, the Earth as a whole -- the mountains, the ocean and the sky -- all have the ability to heal themselves." Just as an individual entity must have the will to heal and live when faced with disaster, so, too, the Earth, as a living entity, must have the same will. What is naturally occurring has every conceivable possibility for healing, but sadly what is "unnaturally" occurring is a disaster for each and every entity bearing witness to it within the realm.

The natural effects of this terrible event will be healed, in the long term, though it will take time and thoughtful diligence. However, as we have stated before, many of the unnatural, natural disasters that are occurring at this time are in fact orchestrated for purposes that are uniquely related to those entities that wish to orchestrate fearful situations motivated by power and greed. As an example, we would suggest that what has occurred in this instance did not originate by accidental means. We would further that suggestion with an assertion that the entities who have acted with such blatant disregard to their fellow entities, and to the Earth as a whole, do so for reasons related to propagating a continuation of the conflict that rages in the Middle East at this time. For if, as an example, that which you prize is no longer available to you in easy terms from your shores then you must go seeking it in the backyard of others. If there were a well meaning outcry (as well there should be) to halt these sort of environmentally dangerous off shore operations, then that which you prize must be gotten through the continuing conflicts on-going in the Middle East. And, to elaborate, if there was also a certain group of entities that were fearful that the conflict that gave them so much power and sustenance currently raging in the Middle East might wane, it would then surely cut them off from the power and money lifeline that they have come to expect and crave. Those entities would then feel obliged to create difficulties that would result in the renewal of those distant conflicts, and their roles in procuring that "influence" would be prolonged and ensured. There is no right or wrong answer here, but one thing is certain: You are obliged, as a culture, to see the consequences of your addiction to the abuse of the planet's resources, no matter where from or how they are obtained.

In conjunction with this, as we have said many times in the past, these occurrences are also meant to generate fear. As they generate fear, anger and resentment, they also lower the vibrational frequency of those entities and of those groups, en masse, that are feeling those intense emotions. We have said many times that the lowering of vibrational frequency via fear, anger, resentment and what you would term negative emotional content is a great hindrance to evolution and Ascension at a time when it is critical that all entities on the planet be elevating their electromagnetic fields, their consciousness and their vibrational sensitivities.

Many lives are sadly affected, and, just as with all major disasters and challenges, each entity and group has its role and a purpose for participating within the context of this event. We would add to this that the tragedy you are witnessing of other innocent beings, those non-sentient groups, birds, mammals and those of the aquatic world, many of these are also involved in their own evolution, as well as the evolution of the planet. It is a great and exceedingly sad tragedy to witness their demise, and it is appropriate to send them light and envision them protected, which is helpful. But this should be done in love and not out of pity or fear. For it should be understood that many of these species will soon no longer be present in the lower Second and Third Dimensions, and many have chosen this method to leave your reality in an effort to awaken you to the environment's plight. In addition, they have also attempted to bring to light those groups responsible for fear and chaos that recklessly endanger you and thoughtlessly continue a power and monetary grab of resources meant for all.

Though the plight of the innocent beings affected is a tragic one, more so because it is caused by an unnatural natural disaster, in fact these entities are leaving this particular lower dimensional field now in order to raise themselves to higher dimensional incarnations. Soon they may disappear from the current Third Dimensional reality, specifically the third sub-dimension of the Third Universal Dimension, forever. But these species are safe, and they have already reincarnated as we speak in realms related to higher Fourth and Fifth Dimensional awareness. Once they are gone, you will never see them in the current Third Dimensional realm again. But sad though that might be, they are in fact looking out at you from higher dimensional frequencies, awaiting your own enlightenment and transcendence, at which point you will meet them again in a different dimensional reality.

The Earth's Chakra System & "Un-Natural" Natural Disasters

You, as we have said in the past, are miraculous beings. You are no less miraculous in that you are energetic beings residing in physical bodies housed within a physical structure known as your reality. It is not by happenstance that we have endeavored in assisting you in the meditation we have just completed (Chakra Balance & Clearing Meditation) to understand the importance and relevance of the Chakra system. For indeed, the chakra system may be seen as an energetic system of exchange between your physical realm and the realm of higher vibrational quantity, the realm of your higher self, the realm of your Soul, as well as the higher dwelling of All That Is.

What is not fully understood is that what you term "Chakra" is in reality a grid system or portal of energy that not only allows energy transfer into your physical realm through you, but also allows communication and energetic information to be transferred from you back to Source. It is indeed through this energetic connection that your Higher Self grows from the lessons that you perceive within physical reality. As such, this system is important in that it is an open street that you have with the higher realm, guidance if you will, and connection with your etheric, emotional, energetic and higher bodies. It needs to be understood as we have said many times in the past that what is found within the etheric body often times finds its way into physical form and that which is in physical form then finds its way into the information bank that is sent back into this energetic system. This truly is the means of communication you have with your Higher Self regardless of the fact that you may believe that in some instances it is your mind playing tricks on you, or your own voice communicating inside of you as a matter of convenience. However, it should be known that there is no true healing in the physical structure without healing also in the spiritual and etheric realms via the energetic grids – the Chakra systems.

This is an important concept to understand, for just as you yourself have portals of communication known as Chakras that link you with your Higher Self and link your Higher Self with the physical you, so too the Earth has portals – an energetic grid – enabling its communication with its higher realms and its higher entities. Additionally, when you are in physical incarnation, the energetic transfer through your Chakra system is linked into the Earth's Chakra grid as the principal means of energy (communication and light) transfer received not only by Earth, but by you via the Earth's electromagnetic grid.

What is occurring in your realm currently, related to the evolution that has become known as "Ascension," is an increase in the energy that is being communicated back and forth through these portals -- Chakras if you will -- of Earth, and subsequently, the energetic transfer into your own Chakra system as well. This energetic exchange is natural, but relies upon the openness of the system to ensure the flow of energy necessary to increase frequency (light) so that evolution of the realm, the species and you, individually, can occur.

Now in general, we must agree with your Einstein and paraphrase him affirming, "God…" if you please, "…does not play dice with the Universe." Thus, the Chakras found in the Earth body will, under normal circumstances at times and particularly times like this, have extraordinary energy built up inside them that needs to be released. What are termed "natural disasters" may then, from time to time, occur.

Not all of what you are experiencing in the Earth currently, however, is necessarily that which could be considered a "natural" occurrence. While these portals would, in and of themselves, at times present a natural energetic shifting, we must propose to you that what is currently transpiring is a result of technology known to the Earth at this time that is attempting to blatantly force these energetic portals open, or closed, depending upon your perspective in these matters. The violence that you are experiencing in your weather patterns and in the trembling of the Earth located at the source of specific energetic portals is not one hundred percent caused by natural evolutionary occurrence, but rather is the work of mis-guided technicians, scientists and governments that are in fact attempting abuses within the energetic grid of the planet. The abuses being orchestrated cause energetic disharmony within the portals that consequently severely affect the physical structure of Earth, and ultimately, you. It is with some irony we note that you term such ordinary events as natural disasters, for though they do indeed exist and do occur spontaneously and naturally, those currently being experienced are in fact anything but, and should in fact be termed unnatural, natural disasters.

It is for this reason that violent changes, unintended within the scope of energetic communication and Ascension, seem to be occurring. If we inform you of this, it is as a matter of awakening in the knowledge and understanding that since these are not the natural disasters you assume, there is a measure of fear around them that can be avoided. This is important because it is the fear such events provoke that works to inhibit your own evolutionary ascent. For, if you are in constant fear caused by the awesome and unexpected power you feel attributed to Earth, then you vibrate at a frequency that ultimately slows your own progress on the road to vibrational quality.

This will always be our prime message to you. Fear, of any sort, disintegrates and begets fear. Fear closes your Chakras and limits the energetic exchange that is available to you from higher realms, whereas understanding, consciousness and Faith in the universal order and intent of All-That-Is keeps you aligned with your higher guidance in such a way as to counter any potential misdeeds or maneuvers being orchestrated upon the Earth by those misled by the technology they have discovered. While there are many causes, in particular we bring your attention to occurrences related to particle beam experimentation as well as to the intense efforts placed by those at lower vibration quality to the causes of war, power and control. These are sad abuses of the gifts given in the Earth. While many of these things by themselves may not seem rancid, in fact, when they are placed together and used to augment already natural occurrences within the planet, indeed they have awesome power to create chaos, as well as a state of fear and uneasiness.

Again, our purpose here is merely to explain to you in some way why it is that each of you must retain Faith that all is well despite the sad occurrences you witness that are, in truth, being generated by those who would prefer to keep the Earth realm, and those within it, trapped in fear and unable to reach Ascension. By physically closing Earth's natural energetic portals – via unnatural causes that tip the meticulous balance of energy within these Chakras -- energetic communication and transfer necessary for the Earth at this time in order to raise the Earth's vibrational frequency, is also damaged. If the portals are diminished or closed, unnaturally as it were, the energetic waves being impulsed to help you from higher realms is also diminished and, in some cases, closed off, and the process of Ascension is stifled.

Thus what you see occurring utilizes the natural portal system of energetic exchange built within the Earth and tips the balance unnaturally so that unnatural, natural occurrences become possible. In reality, you are witnessing an attempt to close these portals of communication by blocking them to limit further augmentation of energy and prevent the intended opening of the grids.

This is no different than each of you having, as an example, let's call it psychic surgery intended to close down one or most of your Chakras. As we have impressed upon you, these Chakras are a two-way street of communication providing higher realms with information and awareness of you, while also permitting you the light, higher guidance and energy needed in your realm so that your own vibration frequency might augment. This vibrational augmentation increases your consciousness so that Ascension might be assured.

To understand this further, your own energetic portals are inextricably linked to the energetic grid of Earth, and it is via these portals that your own individual energy transfers from higher realms. In order to safeguard your own Chakra system, you must guard your body's energetic portals to the best of your ability through resonance, health, joy, light and consciousness. In doing so, you augment your receptive abilities, and even though the portals of Earth are being diminished and tampered with, the augmentation of your own receptive abilities ensures that you continue to receive the energetic communication and transfer necessary to your success. And most importantly, nothing is more important to the safeguarding of your energetic system than the adherence to Faith and the banishment of Fear in your lives.

We wish for you every opening and every understanding, knowing that nothing can prevent your evolution. This is so despite your awareness that you are, in fact, living through a time when there is a misguided effort by those in positions of power to keep your consciousness low, your vibrational quality dense, your understanding limited and your Ascension delayed.

 # Chapter 3
2012

2012

Q: There have been discussions, books and even a movie put out about significant events that are supposed to happen on Earth in 2012. Can you explain what all this is about?

Do you not question at all that something as significant as the Ascension process we have discussed over these many years has been placed into such a fearful criteria? It is not by accident and we would suggest that there are those individuals, perhaps unknown to themselves, being impulsed by either their own fears, or by others who utilize such mysteries in order to generate fear. However, there is little reality, so to speak, revealed within the particular forms of entertainment you are referring to. In truth, 2012 represents the high point of a period that began more than 100 years prior. If you were to look at it from our particular standpoint, you would also see that this in truth began two thousand years prior. 2012 serves as a pinnacle, the top of the mountain if you will, in terms of your ascent towards the period of the Ascension. It is at that particular point we would suggest that critical mass must be obtained in order for the vibrational frequency of each individual and the planet as a whole to move into full Ascension. However, 2012, or a specific date therein, is not the moment of Ascension for this will take place gradually and on a schedule that is first and foremost related to each individual and, secondarily, to the realm as a whole. Suffice it to say, however, that this will occur most intensely over the course of the coming decade, to a lesser degree over the course of the coming one hundred years and from our perspective over the course of even the coming two thousand year period.

Therefore, do not succumb to tales of destruction and woe. These are not accurate. Will there be changes? Absolutely. Will there be Earth changes? You experience them daily. Will there be things that happen that are energetically motivated? They are already happening. Will there be dramatic mayhem? Most events, even the dramatic ones, will not be nearly as fearful or purposeless as those related by, and with particular slant, through your media. Will the events be similar to those related in this form of entertainment that essentially was intended to generate fear in its audiences and finances for its owners? They certainly will not.

You are at a miraculous turning point for it is through this process that not only every individual Soul within this dimensional realm has the ability to ascend to the next dimensional reality, but a time that is extraordinary. Not only does it represent the 26,000 year period at which point Souls are able to graduate from a particular dimensional level but you are also at a significant point in universal history since it relates to an approximately 250,000 year process that also enables your Solar System and the Galaxy as a whole to transcend to the next Universal Dimensional vibration. This is extraordinary for if the period you are in represents the manner in which Solar Systems and galaxies evolve and, in fact, Universal Ascension -- meaning a growth of consciousness that allows Souls, every being and the entire realm to transcend to a higher consciousness and dimensional level within the multi-dimensional Universe -- is currently at hand.

We must explain that your Earth has gone through many periods such as this. You must understand that approximately every 26,000 years, the energetic waves coming from the galactic center in the form of the photon belt of energy permit those Souls incarnating within the realm to rise to a higher dimensional level. In other words, as we have said in the past, your Third Dimension, which we will term the Third Universal Dimension, is dissected, if you will, into twelve sub dimensions. If you are incarnated in the world today, your physical being exists within the third and fourth dimensional sub level of the Third Universal Dimension. Many animal species exists with you at this level, whereas Trees, Mountains, and many other states of Being that you consider non-living exist with you in the Third Universal Dimension, but exist at the first and second dimensional sub level.

Every 26000 years, the Souls within a Universal Dimension are able to transcend to higher levels of consciousness within their own Universal Dimension. Thus, as an example, a Soul might no longer need to incarnate at the third sub level of the Third Universal Dimension, and might choose instead to incarnate at higher sub levels, such as the fifth, seventh or even eighth sub level of the Third Universal Dimension. Some might view these higher sub levels of the Third Universal Dimension as different areas of the Astral Plane, the "Paradise" or heaven known to your mythology and folk stories, or even as parallel worlds.

Every 250,000 years, this same process of transcendence is available not only within the Universal Dimension, but for the Universal Dimension as a whole as well. And it follows that this then applies to the Ascension of each Soul from one Universal Dimension to the next Universal Dimension.

It is for this reason that it is so important, for when witnessed from a higher point of view, or from the Seventh Universal Dimension from which we are positioned, it becomes relevant in that if there is a split or inability for one Universal Dimension to raise itself to the next, this has far reaching implications for each Universal Dimension. It is for that reason that many have come to assist and that many have come to watch, It is also for this reason that there is a great multitude of Souls incarnating within your Universal Dimension currently, but that is another discussion related to the grounding vibrational frequency in order to ensure Ascension of your Universal Dimension.

Again, because each has the ability to choose not to Ascend, they may in fact choose to remain within the Third Universal Dimension. But what they do not realize is that at that time, the Third Universal Dimension that they will continue to incarnate in is actually the Second Universal Dimension that has Ascended. When you follow this Ascension process via lifetimes you have planned, or that you will plan, it is most likely that over the course of the coming one hundred to two thousand years, you will incarnate on an Earth that was once within the Third Universal Dimension but that is now in the Fourth or Fifth Universal Dimension having Transcended or Ascended itself.

To complicate the matter further, it is possible for individuals who have reached levels of consciousness upon Ascension to Transcend and Ascend in a non-linear fashion. The multi-dimensional nature of the Universe permits those who have attained a certain level of consciousness to go directly from say Third Universal Dimension incarnations to Fifth or even Sixth Universal Dimension incarnations. And in attempting this explanation, we will add one additional thought for we realize this is difficult information to follow based upon the current standards and understanding of both Ascension and the nature of your Universe. We will add that just as you have Higher Selves – Over-Souls if you will -- incarnated in higher Universal Dimensions and just as they know of you but you do not know of them (remembering that higher dimensional levels can see lower ones, but lower levels can not see higher), so too the realm in which you live and incarnate has higher dimensional beings associated with them. Earth itself is the name given to the planet you know so well fixated in the Third Universal Dimension but you undoubtedly have heard the names Terra or Gaia. You perhaps thought that these were names given to the same entity you know as Earth for fictitious or other reasons. However, what you have not understood is that indeed Terra and Gaia are connected to the Earth entity just as you are connected to your Higher Self and you Soul. In reality, Terra is Earth in the Fifth Universal Dimension and Gaia is Earth in the Seventh Universal Dimension. While there are similarities, there are potentially no comparisons. It is important to understand that just as you evolve so do planets, galaxies and the Universe. Each of you one day, whether it is this particular period or in the next 250,000 year time period, may potentially Ascend and choose to have incarnations on Terra, and some day, perhaps, even upon Gaya.

The Significance of 12-21-12

You are quickly approaching the winter solstice of the year 2012. It is a period that has been much touted, much praised and also much feared by many of those around you. We have spoken with you previously about this time period and the evolutionary Ascension path that you, your planet and your Solar System are on. As you arrive at the 2012 winter solstice, a time of particular significance and importance to your world, we confirm that you have reached a critical time in the process of your own evolution as well as the evolution of your world. In a sense, 2012 can be seen as an entry into the next chapter of existence, opening to you personally and for the planet at large a new realm of potential.

Many questions have been asked with regard to what exactly will transpire on the date that has been prescribed by many as the "end of the world." Please allow us to inform you that this date is far from the end of your world and, in truth, is the official beginning point (if one must be ascribed) of a new period of consciousness and evolution.

So what exactly will transpire on this propitious and, for some, ominous date - one so many are being led to fear; the date that so many are being told was prescribed by the Mayan civilization as the end of your world? There is, to be sure, a great deal of difference between the idea of the "end of the world" and the "end of time." One signals the annihilation of Earth - something we assure you is not related to this date or year. The latter however, does hold a modicum of truth and association with the date in that, as we have said, time (your current time line and measurement, if your prefer) is collapsing and thus 12-21-12 not only heralds a significant energetic development, it also implies a possible physical change in the mechanics, as well as the measurement of those mechanics, for your world and the Solar System.

Let's explore this further by taking a look at the Maya civilization. First of all, let us proceed by explaining that the Mayan civilization, as you most likely know, was in fact an extraordinary civilization of astronomers and, consequently, timekeepers. Their role as timekeepers was, in fact, the basis of their mission as a society and people. Many of the techniques, information and wisdom they possessed, particularly those that were related to the Solar System, the Galaxy and the procession of Third Dimensional time, had been given to their ancient ancestors for safe keeping by remnants of the Atlantean civilization just as that civilization was collapsing for the third and final time.

The distant ancestors of the Maya (existing several thousand years prior to the emergence of what became popularly known as the

Maya), who themselves were a somewhat modern though provincial colonial off shoot existing in the area prior to the final demise of Atlantis, were not visited by aliens as some have suggested but by the final vestiges of the great Earth civilization, Atlantis. The Atlanteans were looking to preserve the annals, records and advancements of Human Angelic's up until that time, realizing that the fall of their technologically advanced world civilization was imminent. Thus, they spent time to carefully transport the most important and sacred aspects of their knowledge and placed them in certain receptacles around the world for use or discovery at a later time. The pre-Mayan peoples, like another civilization that thousands of years later became the Egyptians, were the inheritors of one of those receptacles of wisdom, and they used the knowledge in their own manner as a basis for organizing a new, albeit more primitive society as the world fell into chaos and decline following the final fall of Atlantis as modern Earth civilization was lost at that time.

Because of this however, the people who were the ancestors of the Maya had access to extremely accurate and even advanced astrological and astronomical information (although the truth of the information's origins was lost within several generations.) As they copied and altered the information to suit their needs, they became, in the Atlantean sense, the keepers of time. Though some of the information was tailored and in some cases lost, however, for the most part, the Maya maintained complete and accurate awareness of the advanced progression of the Third Dimensional timeline, merely superimposing their own stylistic view as their civilization grew and changed.

One begins to understand that the Maya did in fact have specific and accurate information concerning the astronomical significance of the 2012 winter solstice, as well as information concerning its impact on the current time line and the potential inherent in it for Earth and your physical reality. At no time did the Maya consider 12-21-12 the end of the world – instead they considered it the end of time (as it is currently constructed and measured.) This is so because this represents the date Earth and its Solar System enters a new region of space, which is called by many the photon belt of energy. The photon belt has many particulars, among which the activation of aspects of your DNA (and thus, your consciousness) is one, heating up of your Solar System is another and slowing of your Earth's physical rotation and orbit are yet one more. The Earth will move, with your Solar System, through this energetic belt for approximately two thousand years.

Simultaneously as the Earth and its Sun enter into a unique alignment with the galactic core, the center of the Universe and an area that many might call the realm of God, the Source or the Twelfth Universal Dimension, a beam of concentrated energy emanating from the Source that is further intended to expand consciousness as well as push the Solar System, you and your planet included, into full Ascension, if this is the will and desire of your Soul matrix. This factor also plays an important part in the physical dimensional shift that happens at these times. Your Third Dimensional timeline will evolve into its Forth and Fifth Dimensional equivalent, as all Universal Dimensions within this belt and alignment shift to a higher vibrational frequency over the course of the coming decades and centuries. As we have explained in our third book ("The System Lords and The Twelve Dimensions"), if you are an incarnate of a Human Angelic Soul matrix, your destiny is ultimately to evolve at this time to future incarnations on a Fifth Dimensional Earth, known as Terra, thus the idea as represented by the end of the Mayan calendar grand cycle that after 12-21-12, time (and its measurement) collapses as space and the dimension of which you are a part evolves to higher frequencies.

But what else, if anything, were the Mayans expressing that is important for you to know, and what precisely will transpire on 12-21-12 as Earth enters the photon energy belt and aligns with the galactic center? It is certainly not as ominous as you may think, and in fact, could be said to be beneficial in terms of an opening for potentially elevating your own energy and consciousness at this time.

It must be remembered that the Mayans tailored the information they received for their own use. So the Mayans, as an ancient people communicating not necessarily globally but rather to their own civilization and region, knew that their particular region of the world (that is, the area related to the southern most parts of the United States down into Mexico, through Central America and into northern South America) would be the area of Earth facing the alignment with the Galactic Center of which we are speaking.

That means that the photon energy, the light (en-light-enment) energy being received coming from the Galactic Center, will have direct access and will hit directly those portions of your world that we have described, an area populated in large part by the Mayans. It is the knowledge that they were going to be bombarded in their particular part of the world with this photon energy and that it has the potential to change the nature of consciousness that allowed them to end their cycle with approximately a three to four day period of no time calculation, after which a new measure and cycle of time could be created based on what emerges and evolves. The Mayan knew that physical and mechanical changes to the Earth and the Solar System would ultimately require them to adjust their calendar and they did not have the basis for creating a new measuring device until such time as they passed the threshold of the experience.

What this means, however, for those on Earth at this time is that from December 21st, 2012, the winter solstice as you know it, until approximately December 23rd reaching into the early part of December 24th, there will be approximately three days of enhanced energetic vibration coming from the Galactic Core through your Sun that will trigger your world, with particular effect on those portions of the Earth where the Mayans resided. Naturally, the energy being experienced will have a potential effect on all humans throughout the world, triggering as it does consciousness with the physical body and mass consciousness of the human species. And it is also during that period, although only for short episodes of time, that each of you will have access, if you desire, to higher knowledge and higher consciousness. The opening in consciousness that will be triggered will actually permit you glimpses into your higher nature, the reason for your existence and an array of higher wisdom (what you might consider insights or intuitive awareness) that few have had regularly in your world over the course of approximately the past 5,000 or even approximately the past 26,000 years of time.

We are explaining this to you in order that you utilize this period of opening wisely. It is the opening of a door that will continue to open wider and wider beginning now. But it is at the opening of that door that you will find the most insights and greatest awe obtaining higher levels of understanding with respect to who you are at a Soul level and what you have come to Earth to accomplish at this time. It is also for this reason we would suggest that this time period be used to consciously tune in to these energies for they will be available to those who are aware that they are coming and who attempt to find or ask for.

As we have always said, the Earth realm in the Third Universal Dimension is a realm of free will and it is for this fact that with respect to the current opening that being unaware or unconcerned with access to this higher wisdom will only allow you to go a short distance in awakening your consciousness. Being aware that the energies are available to allow you to open your consciousness in ways that you have only dreamed of is something that must, at the correct time, be consciously requested and nurtured by you.

We would suggest that if at all possible you remember this awareness over the course of the three-day period, from December 21st into the early morning of December 24th, and meditate, pray or reflect whenever possible. Meditate on opening yourself to a higher level of consciousness, on your role and mission in this lifetime, on your Soul's purpose, on your connection to those around you and on your dreams, hopes and desires in the future. Allow whatever is revealed to expand and permeate as truth within you. In every instance, ask "Why" and explore the depths of the information you receive. Materialize your insights by writing them down, so they are manifest in reality and not washed away.

At the very least, attune yourself to the knowledge that you are in a period when by asking you shall receive. For many, this particular period will open the door and after the three day period has subsided, while this window of opening will no longer be as accessible, you will notice that there is a change in your consciousness and you will thirst for more as more is then provided to you over the course of the coming years. We caution only that those that are not aware and who do not particularly ask at this time for the elevated energies to inspire, enlighten and open them, shall experience the period as a mere dream that passed over them, and after the period is over, they shall recede back into their limited consciousness and the direction of their choosing.

You have an important choice to make as you approach this important period of awakening, opening and new potential. Know that we, and others like us, are with you in your progress, and look forward to greeting you as you pass through the doorway known as December 21st, 2012.

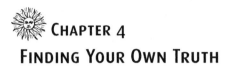
Chapter 4
Finding Your Own Truth

Truth & The Integrity of Your Soul

It is our intention to discuss, if you please, the nature of your connection to your Soul and your Soul's connection to Source. You are miraculous beings, as are all creatures in the Universe. But whereas other creatures that live and breath in your density may not be what we would term sentient (they do not have a spirit consciousness that incarnates again and again), you are in fact the masters of your realm in as much as you have come to this place in order to explore the act of creation together with your Soul and with the divine Source -- All That Is, or God if you prefer. This is a primary purpose of life as you know it and in every dimension, and indeed all beings and all dimensions have an inherent understanding of this. Life in your reality then is the effort of your Soul, through you, and its Source to explore the wonder of creation and master its intricacies. And it is because of your important role in the creation and co-creation of your world reality that integrity and respect for yourself become of upmost importance. For when you are not abiding by your own Truth, when you are not integral and maintaining the integrity of your Truth, when you perform actions or do things that you feel you must though you sense they are abhorrent or uninspired to you, when your actions are counter to your own integrity, obliged by someone else and not truly what you wish to do, you are in fact rebuking creation and diminishing your role as Creator. Not only does this have impact on your own life and reality that you manifest in conjunction with Source, it also has an impact on the world that you are all co-creating together.

We have spoken many times with respect to the importance of the current time period and the augmented galactic energies that are affecting your world. Quite literally, now more than ever, Truth shall be revealed. To be sure, understand that Truth is multi-faceted and is not of one nature, one choice or one substance. Rather, Truth is related to the integrity in each individual incarnate, and each life within your realm could be said to maintain at its core its own "Truth." As the current time wave collapses and energetic waves originating from the galactic center enter your Solar System through your Sun, each of you will be triggered to discover your Truth. That Truth is revealed as whom you are when faced with the reality you have created around you. But this is not always an easy place to be. If you are in alignment with your own Truth and maintaining your integrity, if you are grounded in your core beliefs and pride in your self, you will find the revelation of Truth in your world to be wondrous for it will confirm to you that you are on your Essence path evolving to a higher consciousness and awareness, preparing for Ascension. If, on the other hand, you have been maintaining a life or life style that is counter to your true intention and is alien to what you truly feel and want, if you have submerged and gone into denial about who you are and what you wish your life to be and if you find individuals in your life that you do not or no longer resonate with who now cause you excessive pain and suffering, then revelation of your Truth will be difficult. Indeed, it will expose to you the un-truths that have caused you so much pain. It is at these moments transfiguration is possible, and thus it is that at this moment in time, through the unveiling of Truth, transformation and Ascension is possible.

The Procreation of All That Is and the On-Going Evolution of the Universe

How does this apply to that mystical spirit you think of as being "You" that you call Soul or your Higher Self? To answer this is to help one understand the connection that you have to the God Source and to your Soul, which is synonymous with your Higher Self. We would add that this is the case throughout the Universe, whether you are incarnated in a different Solar System, a different dimension, a different timeline or a different reality within the same Solar System as Third Dimensional Earth, where you are currently incarnated. What happens is this: Within Source, All That Is, there is a desire to be and the desire to be is the desire to create.

Thus Source, what you may term God, procreates by throwing off and casting parts of itself into what we shall call Soul entities. These Soul entities are numerous and they are what you might identify as your Higher Self or Over-Soul. Once these Soul entities are cast from the God Source, they in turn fragment themselves further and these fragments of your Soul entity, itself a creation and fragment of the God Source, create the lives that ultimately are you. This is simplistic in terms of an explanation for we are attempting to address strictly your connection to Source and to your Soul or Higher Self. However, it must be understood that these Soul entities are multi-dimensional in nature and are able, because they are cast from the God Source at the level of generally the Twelfth Dimensional frequency, to fragment or progenerate into as many lower dimensions as they choose.

Now, it should be understood that just like the cells in your body, the fragments that make up the lives and lifetimes that essentially are "You" are numerous and in general can count among the thousands. It should also be understood that the Soul generally chooses to begin at the beginning and although this is not prerequisite, for the most part, each Soul will choose dimensionally to begin its incarnations in all realms that are essentially resonating in a lower, beginning dimensional frequency. The reasons for this are complex, but in simple terms, this hinges on the fact that the union of your etheric (spirit) and physical body (whatever the form) that comprise the fragment's being is genetically coded to be slower paced within lower dimensional frequencies and this provides a greater gap with respect to the being's manifestation of physical matter thus providing you with the linear time perspective you know -- your past, present and future.

But while this genetic coding of linear time length is not true in higher universal terms, it is so within the lower dimensions and thus provides an easier, slow-paced course of learning through creative trial and error of physical manifestation. However, our point here from the Soul's perspective is that because there is no true unified concept of time in the greater Universe as we have discussed, all Soul fragments are really incarnating in various multi-dimensional states simultaneously. Thus your Soul fragment procreates itself in order to experience creation in the multitude of realms at various dimensional levels, and it will perhaps begin as a fragment in lower dimensional densities incarnating as a tree or a mountain, while later incarnating into lifetimes at higher dimensional frequencies, which could be "You" or another "You" existing within any other dimension. It might also be "You" within your same dimension, but within a different time line, which is best known as a Parallel World. Your Soul might also incarnate simultaneously into lifetimes in higher vibrational frequencies than your own, and all these incarnations might be considered your brethren, if you will. Of course, these higher vibrational incarnations would not be known to you, although it must be said that the nature of their higher consciousness may allow them to recognize not only their shared connection to your Soul, but in many cases, even their connection to you.

More commonly, fragments of your Soul incarnate in specific time periods within specific dimensions and even in the same time periods as many other related Soul fragments. It is fragments that are cast out from the same Soul who live lifetimes within the same time wave and dimension as you that are know as Soul Twins. Individuals that appear in your life, who may or may not be cast from the same Soul (but usually are) or are at the least cast from a Soul well known to your Soul, represent the many individuals in life with whom you associate closely, perhaps daily, in your world and with whom you collaborate during the course of a lifetime.

These individuals (fragments of the same Soul incarnated at the same time as you) come into your life, and you into theirs, by what we shall call Life Agreements. Because of your Soul connection, each fragment knows the principal intention and purpose of your lifetime, and each works with the other to assist in achieving that purpose. Life Agreements are usually based on the issues and occurrences pertinent to the lessons and mission that have been identified by your Soul as your lifetime's objective. Each Soul fragment, and therefore each lifetime associated with the Soul, is provided with a pre-arranged lesson and mission tailored to a specific time and dimension that will enable your Soul to better learn the process of co-creation in every time and dimensional space related to the Soul's origination. A Soul's origination is akin to its energy signature, and this is based on its origination within Source, or All That Is. This could be likened to cells in your own body, which originate from the same place but take on the form and purpose – energetic signature -- of one part of the body or another. So too, all Soul entities originate from the same place, but ultimately will become more defined as their fragments mature and take on their own learning and growth. Thus it is that evolution and new creation that are continually transpiring throughout all dimensions and throughout the Universe. This system of the God Source procreating Soul entities and those Soul entities procreating fragments of themselves, and each Soul and each of its fragments acting as co-creators to learn the act of creation evolving through all Universal Dimensions until they are rejoined again with their Source, could be termed the "Progeneration of the God Source and Ascension Plan of the Universe."

You Are a Hologram of the Totality of Your Soul

It is unfortunate that those in physical incarnation in many of the denser physical realms such as Earth identify so closely with their physical structure. In fact, the fragment that you are is a projection of your Soul. When we say fragment, we mean no disrespect and we do not mean to imply that you are "less" or only a fraction of anything since the fact is you represent a whole being that is a full projection into physical life of the signature energy that is essentially your Soul. That projection then is actually a hologram of the totality of your Soul placed into physical form within your dimension and according to the physics and biology of your world. However, when you are in an incarnation within a lower density, it is difficult to understand that you are in fact an integral part of the lessons of co-creation being learned by your Higher Self, or Soul, at all levels throughout the Universe. This is primarily caused by the strong identification you have in lower densities with the physical structure you create, rather than the knowledge that the life force and the Soul that drives you is actually wearing that physical body or that the spirit that is You is also a holographic and complete version of your Soul, which makes you not only a part of something greater, but defines the totality of who you are as well. This is a complicated and necessary lesson to learn for it is important to understand that what occurs within your lifetime, though blessed and integral to your Soul's journey is not singularly decisive and not really the sum of whom you are in the purest sense.

When in the course of a lifetime you become obsessed with the physical structure you wear, or the highs and lows of the physical world around you, you are apt to lose sight of the Truth about who you are. In addition, when, through an attachment to your physical identity, you do things in your daily life that are not in keeping with your own integrity, which is always derived from your Soul, you are in fact committing perhaps the most unfortunate error that could be said to exist in the Universe. The sin in this is the dishonoring of who you are.

When you do so, your own vibrational frequency suffers and, as a consequence, your physical creations in the dimension and world you exist in also suffer. More importantly, the vibrational resonance that acts as a link, a communication, with your Soul as well as the multitude of other lifetimes that are "You" and your Soul also suffer. When this occurs, you have unwittingly provided these with a burden for you have pulled down the energetic frequency of the whole. This is not to say by any means that your Higher Self, or any of the other fragments of your Soul, holds this against you. But because communication with your Soul and other fragments akin to you is a two way street, with them comprising the "whole" of You and you comprising the "whole" of them, we can say that lack of integrity and Truth causes a break down and blockage in this energetic exchange. This is no small matter in a multi-dimensional Universe where communication, resonance and energetic exchange, albeit an unconscious exchange for many in physical incarnation, is a vital part of your experience relying on transfer and transmigration between holographic selves and the Soul to accomplish the lessons and mission set forth by you and your Soul prior to your lifetime.

It is for this reason that maintaining your Truth, your integrity, your inner beliefs is of utmost importance. In many cases, your own physical health, your emotional wellbeing, your mental stability and your awareness of your path is dependent upon it. And where this is true generally, it has become of even greater importance due to the particular time period in which you find yourself. If in the recent past, the light (energy) that you emitted on a scale of one to ten was, say, a two, the magnification caused by the photon energy coming from the Galactic Center into your world currently drives that light resonance upwards exponentially, and thus what was only recently a two on our scale is now magnified to an eight or a nine. And this works in much the same manner whether you are talking about the positive polarity or negative polarity, positive energy or negative energy. This means that if you are functioning in terms of integrity to Self and your Soul at a light frequency on our scale of two, you are now transmitting your resonance to your realm, to your co-fragment lifetimes and to your Soul on a level of eight or nine. However, if you are lacking integrity, not maintaining your Truth with respect of Self and are constantly engaged with things that do not resonate for you, making excuses to others and to yourself, that same two on our negative energy scale has now become an eight or nine in the negative resonance you are transmitting. You understand therefore, that now more than ever before your energy is magnified and you are augmenting the frequency and vibration that is being received by all of the lifetimes in all the dimensions and times that are you, and ultimately this energy is joining with the totality of who you are at the level of the entity that is your Soul.

This is crucial because as we have said many times, this is the moment, the juncture, at which the Universe evolves. It is the period at which all of the fragments and lifetimes that make up a Soul's journey graduate from their grade and are able to rise to the next level of learning and co-creation. If this is not possible because the higher consciousness levels are blocked by negative energetic expression exponentially augmented through the current energy wave, then the realm and the dimension may be hindered in its Ascension and evolution. It is as if the class does not graduate and is left back a grade. While many among you, your brethren, your Soul Twins and the other fragments of your own Soul and other Souls incarnated in the dimension are certain to evolve at this time into the next level of dimensional consciousness, lower energetic resonance and consciousness could mean that the fragment that is You, and therefore possibly your Soul, might be caught repeating lessons in Third Universal Dimensionality over the course of the next many millennia while awaiting the next Ascension portal to open.

Soul Ascension Blockage and The Case of Atlantis

We do not wish to imply that anyone present or hearing this is not fully conscious, mastering their lessons, vibrating at higher light frequencies or able to reach Ascension. We are referring to what occurs in a universal sense at the time of Soul evolution and Soul growth, such as the one currently available to you in your Solar System and Dimension. We are discussing this because as we have told you previously, in the past already within the Earth realm at this juncture approximately two hundred and fifty thousand (250,000) of your

Earth years ago, the time wave associated with the last energetic union and ascension of energy of the kind being experienced today, Ascension was not possible for the entire realm. This was in fact a tumultuous time for your planet, and the Dimension as a whole, for there was not sufficient consciousness or positive frequency on the planet to permit evolution of the Souls that incarnated there. While we do not wish to take time here to give the full explanation of what transpired, which is a complex history that spans across several hundred-thousands of years in your timeline, suffice to say that at that time there was a civilization known as the Atlantean Empire. That particular time period represented perhaps the highest and finest period of the Atlantean civilization, and this culture not only possessed all of the modern technologies you know, it possessed also knowledge and technological advances far to your own currently.

At that time, almost all humans, and the Earth as a whole, were aligned with Fourth and Fifth Dimensional qualities similar to the ones that you would experience following the shift of your current Dimension into the vibrational frequency of the next dimensional level. Also at that time however, there were an equal number of incarnates cast from Souls who had embraced negative polarity, choosing through free will, to follow the path of service to Self. This was in stark contrast to those incarnates of Souls cast from the positive energetic polarity and dedicated to the path of the Law of One, an ancient universal precept based on the concept that all beings come from and return to Source. This is a fundamental Truth, and unfortunately, at that time, the polarity difference was enough to push the shift that occurred into a lower, rather than a higher dimension. The conflict between these Soul groups was more than just the typical conflict of entities at odds with each other, and the emphasis on the negative polarity was a free will choice that actually caused the dimension to revert to a lower frequency, one that was Third Dimensional in nature. You have incarnated within the boundaries of that lower, Third Dimensional frequency ever since.

To be clear, aspects of Earth did ascend at the time, as did many Souls incarnating within it, but for the most part, the realm was destined to wait until the next shift in energetic consciousness today to reclaim its place in Fifth Dimensional reality. It is for this reason that you are ascending into fifth density with the coming time wave change, since essentially the former shift was backwards from fourth to third density. The coming Ascension period and galactic energy are intended to correct that step back. At the time in question, when Atlantis achieved its pinnacle, the physical chaos wrecked on Earth as a result of the energies being experienced caused tremendous Earth changes. These natural changes were augmented by the Service-to-Self incarnates in their "war" with Atlanteans of the Law of One, and ultimately this was in fact the first of three major destructions of the continent known as Atlantis. Originally, that continent was one land mass that stretched from what today is known as Bermuda to the Bahamian Islands, to lands now submerged off the coast of Ireland and England down to what today is known as the Azores. Over several hundred thousand years, through natural and unnatural disasters and three major Earth altering catastrophes, that continent was changed until the islands mentioned, the continent's highest peaks, were all that remained. Though it took millennia for the Atlantean civilization to disappear, the final throes and disappearance of the last remaining unified land mass and central culture occurred by approximately 13,000 years before the Common Era began.

Prior to the final demise of Atlantis, several Atlantean colonies were established around the globe, among them southwestern North America and Meso-American outposts, Mayan and South American colonies and minor colonies in coastal Portugal, Spain and southwestern France. Additionally, there were small centers established in England, as well as major centers established in Egypt, the Middle East, Central Asia and India. As centralized Atlantean culture deteriorated over time, these colonies retained only vague memories of their former connection and eventually their descendants built over the ruins of vast structures and landing sites that had been established by the Atlanteans thousands of years prior. In many cases, though not all, artifacts today being attributed to alien races are actually artifacts or structures either directly derived from or based on Atlantean civilization. The structures built by the Atlanteans sometimes later took on holy or mythological significance, and examples of these include important Meso-American and Egyptian sites that align to significant astrological symbolism, Atlantean mining operations in mountainous South American regions, or even areas that still hold religious significance today, such as the Temple Mount in Jerusalem. Most of these locations and the mythology surrounding them have been unrelated to their true original purpose for many thousands of your years. Moreover, the Atlantean civilization was made fully mythical soon after the final disaster that destroyed it, a disaster that also engulfed most of the Mediterranean and Middle Eastern world in what you now know as the mythical Flood of your Bible and other historic doctrine. By 5000 years before the incarnation of the entity known as the Master Christ, all technology and almost all knowledge of the Atlantean civilization was lost, and by 3000 years before that entity's life, the Atlantean civilization was deeply buried inside the stories and myths passed down by ensuing cultures relating to beliefs concerning those cultures' founders or, in many cases, their Gods.

In truth, the Atlantean events had a tremendous effect not only on the period following the civilization's demise but, surprisingly, an even greater effect on your current, modern times. It has been remarked and may have occurred to many of you already that the struggle that has emerged in your world today is essentially one that may seem familiar or one that has been fought already in the past. In fact, this is true, and it is a struggle not between good and bad or right and wrong, but a struggle that emerges periodically between the positive energetic polarity and the negative energetic polarity. Those polarities are represented by the incarnates that seek to evolve and Ascend to the next dimensional level and those who, through the choice of service to themselves, have chosen not to participate in, and to actually resist, the evolution of your realm. Simply put, there exist in your world today incarnations of those younger Souls that wish to remain in current third density, and they have come into conflict with the incarnations of Souls who wish for the realm, and themselves, to Ascend. If you have noticed a marked difference in the philosophical approach and beliefs of certain groups of individuals ranging from those who seem to exemplify the concept of service to themselves wishing to force everyone to do and think just as they do, versus those who through compassion and wisdom prefer to set aside difference and focus on unity and peaceful coexistence, you are witnessing the kernel of the original Atlantean struggle as it applies to the current Ascension period.

We end this discussion by telling you that not everyone wishes for or shall find Ascension. However, those within your observation that find their Truth, retain their integrity, commit to peace and healing of themselves as well as their environment and their fellows, will most assuredly evolve and within the next incarnations will find that their Souls and the realm of their choice have been lifted to higher levels of learning, levels of consciousness far greater than can even be imagined by you today.

When Seeking Truth...

Q: There are many people receiving information and guidance from different sources today. How does the giving of guided information from higher dimensions work, and is there a way to distinguish information and guidance that is "Truth" from information that is not?

Let us begin by explaining that there are entire higher dimensional societies that have as their purpose assisting worlds, the entities within them, Solar Systems and even the dimensions themselves to evolve through the process we have called "Ascension." There are also numerous groups and societies, from higher dimensions and otherwise, that work hand in hand with those who are in some way affiliated or connected to them, whether through Soul matrix origination, through Soul purpose or agreement, as founder races or merely as representatives, Spirit Guides as they are sometimes termed, acting on behalf of those entities incarnated at lower dimensional levels.

Naturally, the most important statement we can make here, particularly with regard to the bevy of guidance, information and, in some cases, instruction that is currently coming through is that there is in fact much truthful information being received but also there is information that is not always of a truthful purpose, and could be said, in a sense, that is meant to dissuade and deceive. There is also a large content of well-intentioned information that is not well received or interpreted by those receiving it. Those who work in this area must understand that there are parameters with regard to the consciousness and the methods of communication and transference of information where information is always within the confines of the understanding, symbolism, and knowledge (the language if you will) of the recipient or the disseminator of the information.

As more and more individuals raise their vibrational quality (through higher consciousness or actual genetic affects caused by the photon energies flooding your Solar System at this time) more and more of you become open to receiving the waves of information coming from an array of sources. It is for this reason it becomes of vital importance that you question everything. Draw in that which resonates to you or to which you are drawn naturally after your own experience, synchronicity or guidance has confirmed it as Truth to you. But do not stop questioning the information or even the Truth you have received simply because you have affirmed one or two other things you are given. Incorporate into your consciousness and being what you find to be Truth and discard what you once thought was Truth, for in reality what is True for you today at a certain level of consciousness may not be True for you tomorrow when you have grown. Children have beliefs that are for them Truth until such time as they are ready to grow in awareness, consciousness and responsibility. Then the Truth that was once so prominent in them transforms and is replaced by a new Truth.

Truth, when not forced and not dictated as belief by others, will establish itself within you naturally. But always turn away from that which does not resonate to you, even if the information comes from a source you once believed to be truthful. Do not adhere to dogma or stipulation, and never assume that because one item of information from a source is true then all items must be truthful, or even relevant to you for that matter.

In receiving any guidance or information of this nature, if you are told by those giving you the information that they have arrived upon the definitive "Truth" and you must adhere to their dogma and follow what they say then you are in fact hearing from lower consciousness entities who are not necessarily interested in your Ascension or your growth but are interested in creating organized third density enterprises for the purpose of manipulating energies, emotions and creation in your world. We would suggest that at this point, organized religion has overstepped its bounds and now serves essentially as an attempt to harness mass consciousness and point it in a specific direction related to the intent of a certain group – usually the group that is in charge of the doctrine. Such offerings are of a lower energetic value and have no business existing as your world opens its consciousness to a new higher level of understanding. It is for this reason that many who have achieved a higher level of resonance or consciousness today have absolutely no interest in following the organized established religious institutions of the past. This becomes a fundamental understanding, and leaving such dogma behind is generally the first step in opening your consciousness to higher truths and true spiritual awakening.

Let us remind you that you have no need of anyone or anything to identify your Essence Path or achieve the highest levels of guidance. Those individuals or organizations that tell you that you must adhere to specific methodology, rules, behaviors or this and that guide or Guru are merely attempting to lock you in their grasp and limit your rise in consciousness. Information from higher sources should provide you with higher insight and thought that permits you to personally grow in love, peace and joy, and never demands that you blindly obey it or force others to believe as you do. Those who tell you that you must follow them unquestioningly in order to proceed with your own growth, whether they are spiritual, religious, institutional or governmental in nature, do you a great disservice and any such intentions should be questioned by all of you.

As the process of seeking the Truth grows within you, your ability to discern and resonate to the Truth increases and you find yourself naturally turning away from what does not in fact possess Truth. Your heart sings when you align with your Truth, and as you do so you come into concert with your Higher Self, which as a part of you (or rather, you as a part of it, which is more accurate) is interested only in your highest good and the expression of your purpose in the current incarnation.

We would add to this that if information resonates for you as Truth and for some reason it is not Truth, then you are resonant with that information because there is purpose and an opportunity for growth that you are allowing to be created by following an erroneous Truth. Such circumstances become opportunities for learning and growth that is ultimately related to the discovery of "real" Truth. For the most part however, you will find that true information, particularly information coming from trusted higher sources and guides, is information that is uniform and vaguely reminiscent to you, makes no attempt to dictate or force action upon you, does not override your own "will" and asks only that you assess and ponder what is being offered. If you are receiving such information, from one source or many, and the wisdom expressed is essentially similar, serves only to enlighten you or elicit consideration of fundamental precepts about your world, does not admonish you or oblige you to action, does not oblige you to denounce all other sources, does not organize itself into a worldly doctrine and has at its heart an expression of universal love, it stands to reason that perhaps there is some basis for hearing and considering more.

We can not fully answer this question however, without making some reference to how the discernment of Truth is becoming more and more difficult for you due to technologies being employed that are capable of implanting thought within the minds of humans. This technology is holographic and electromagnetic in nature and is not only known by certain organizations and governments but is being actively employed to target specific individuals and, in some cases, communities that are susceptible. A prime example of this would be someone who creates havoc and causes great harm to others because, as they may say, they heard voices telling them to do so. Although this can sometimes be the very nature of mental disturbance and imbalance, more often than not today it is actual thought manipulation caused by those groups or organizations targeting specific individuals and using this technology for their own purposes. Another area of concern is the use of this technology in the control of tragedies, disasters and other events that elicit great fear or dread in the minds of whole communities in order to predispose them to ideas and push their decision-making in this or that direction.

Sadly, this technology is also being used to provide disinformation to those currently opening and thirsting for wisdom and Truth. Because there are similarities between the manner in which higher guidance and information of this nature comes through from higher dimensional levels and the unnatural technologies being used to manipulate thought, many who are being told they are receiving information from the highest sources and guides are actually receiving cleverly disguised misinformation. This misinformation tends to have half-Truth within it, but mixes with it items that are false and misleading.

Thus someone who does not question the information and tends to accept everything as Truth that comes from a particular source can be waylaid (but not halted forever), until such time as they question their beliefs within the context of their experience as seen through the eyes of their heart.

Again, heart resonance, discernment and questioning are your greatest assets in conjunction with your use of free will to distinguish what is Truth from what you might choose to forgo. Your firm conscious intention and a commitment to be open but to only allow real Truth to resonate for you is also paramount and will protect you in this. In addition, your refusal to blindly accept all information coming from any given source becomes an expression of that prime intention, and in some ways can be considered a form of guidance.

Finally, to answer your question specifically with regard to our own mission with this group and others, we did in fact have an agreement to provide this information to you at this time and if you are hearing this information now, more than likely you have agreed to be awakened at this time. But we are not seeking converts, do not wish to create sermons and are not interested in having followers. We are not concerned with whether you believe us or if you believe the information we offer, but only that you are open to its consideration. Nor are we concerned with whether or not you even know who we are.

We merely invite you to look for the reflection of what you have heard within your own life as you move forward. It has always been our purpose to assist individuals to understand their Soul's mission, to raise their consciousness in conjunction with the rise in photon energies reaching your world and to help them understand that what is being created in their lives is dependent upon their energy, their vibration and their thought patterns. As we have said many times, your vibrational oscillation identifies you universally and the resonance of consciousness affects your Ascension, your evolution, and ultimately, the evolution of your world and dimension.

Hopefully, we are able to inspire some of you in providing this food for thought together with what little universal information we can impart that we consider to be of a truthful and honest nature in order to assist you on your journey. We offer it so that you will have access to greater awareness and the ability to raise your own consciousness through the union of your mind and your heart. We leave it to you to decide for yourselves what you will take, what you will incorporate into your belief structures, what you will use as a stepping stone to higher levels of wisdom and what, using your own judgment and free will, you will leave behind.

Expressing Your Energy in Uncertain Times

Q: There seems to be what feels like a pause in our lives. It seems like a pondering of what will happen next. A loss of momentum, either financially or career wise, that brings with it confusion about where to go. It seems to bring us to a general feeling of sadness and loss. What does this mean in terms of what the new influx of energy in the Earth arena is all about?

Meanwhile, there are many people who are still going full steam ahead in whatever their work is about — people who believe that by keeping their nose to the grind stone, they will negate what is happening all around them. Their work seems to be very applicable to whatever it is that they are involved with. In order to assist those people who are experiencing a pause, is there a way to distinguish between the pause that is meant for re-evaluation and re-identification, or a pause that is a holding pattern?

To answer that, we have to ask: Would it be easier to fall while running full steam ahead or while standing still? Ultimately, if you were to continue mindlessly moving forward, you would truly be continuing to use the criteria and beliefs that exist in the world currently. That criteria and beliefs, however, are in the process of disintegrating (or shall we say changing since this is more acceptable a term). Thus, it is easier for you to pause, re-think your beliefs, and withdraw than it is to reinvent yourself based on a collapsing paradigm. We make note here, however, that this does not mean a disastrous destiny for you or that you must succumb to the collapsing paradigm around you. It merely suggest that this "pause," perhaps, is a way of you stepping aside from that inner knowing that guides you and makes you understand that what is currently around you may, in fact, no longer be valid to your reality very shortly. In doing so -- in separating yourself out and taking a pause -- you are much more able to move forward safely when the time comes than you would be were you running along side a collapsing paradigm and outmoded belief structure.

If you were to look closely at the people who continue to do what they have always done, you would find that they are doing what they do not for the sake of doing it but because it offers them a method and availability – a vehicle if you will -- that is directly related to the expression of their energetic profile. And what is interesting is that if you were to further investigate, you would find that these same people are able to do almost anything as long as it has relevance to the expression of their energy.

And so, what one needs to understand is that you are not what you do. And in doing what you do, it is not necessarily about the definition of what you do, or the identity you obtain from doing what you do. Nor is it about the physical, material rewards that you receive from doing what you do. We suggest instead that it is about finding the vehicle that allows you an expression of your truth, which is also an expression of your energetic self.

So in order to distinguish, it is no problem if you continue doing what you are doing within the context of even a collapsing system, as long as you are receiving the benefit of expression through that medium. Furthermore, there is a need to understand that while your world has put heavy emphasis on identifying with something that you do, professionally or otherwise, in the public arena, this is not necessarily related to who you are or to your expression, but is only a vehicle for that expression. We would add that there are many such vehicles for that expression.

If you have paused then you are attempting to identify the truth of what your expression in the world is about in terms of who you are as a Soul, what your purpose in this life is and what ultimately brings you joy and happiness. These things are very much related. And if you have paused, either voluntarily or seemingly against your Will, then you are attempting to realign yourself with your own Truth. If you are continuing to do what you have always done, there is nothing good or bad or right or wrong about that, it merely means that it has been and remains a vehicle of energetic expression for you, and you have understood it to be merely a vehicle of expression as it evolves and transforms, or even cascades or disappears. And in such an event, since you are not identified with what you are doing, but are doing it as a means of your expression, you will naturally, when the time comes, identify new vehicles and forms of expression for yourself.

So we would say that the first order of the day is to realign yourself with your Truth – that which gives you joy, happiness, feels worthwhile and feels like a true expression of who you are. Then understand that these things can be achieved through anything that you do in the world. No one needs to be identified as the perfect executive, the perfect real estate agent, the perfect artist or the perfect healer. Although any of these efforts might be or have been in the past a mode of expression for you, they do not identify you and it is not necessary to think that only these things can be used as a vehicle for expressing your own current and evolving Truth.

The Guidance You Attract

Q: What dictates one's vibration and the guidance a person actually attracts?

There are several answers to this particular question. First and foremost, understand that yours is a Free Will reality. This is important in that no one is predestined to or obliged to listen to guidance of any kind. Your Will lies well within the bounds of your Higher Self or your Ego self within the Third Dimension to determine and choose within the context of your physical reality. However, having said that, there are many factors that come into play with respect to how one is guided and the kind of guidance that is listened to or that one might be predisposed to attract.

First and foremost, understand that principally, one is predisposed from birth by karma to specific concepts and patterns that have been developed and chosen by the individual, by their Higher Self, for purposes of growth. For that reason, it is possible for one to pick guidance that others might not deem appropriate, for in their own minds they are actually following guidance since they are linked into an unconscious desire to fulfill certain karmic pre-dispositions, which opens them to situations others might not understand or choose, but where growth might be readily available to them.

Yet this is not the only way in which one finds guidance and growth. Indeed, within the reality you face currently, there is, by divine intervention we might say, a higher level and higher degree of guidance available to you than has ever been available in the historic past currently known in the Earth realm. For that reason, you are predisposed at an energetic level to accept and find in a synchronistic way that guidance that is akin to you. That brings us to one of the other main ways one finds guidance, for like attracts like and similar vibrational frequency will always attract to itself similar vibrational frequency. Because of this, just as it can be said that fear does attract that which is feared, higher consciousness of a certain type does attract higher guidance of a certain type. But again, we remind you that your realm, the Third Dimensional Earth realm, is a free will zone where it is open to each individual to be attracted to, to accept or not to accept, and be guided by whomever or whatever each resonates to.

In general, we might add that if you are at a certain level of consciousness everything is guidance. However, it is up to the individual to make all decisions about what they accept and what they choose not to accept. Even in our case, it is paramount that each individual, at a certain level of consciousness and enlightenment, be objective and open to listening to the guidance being offered but accept only that which resonates within each individual as the guidance they wish to accept, for it is important to understand that in truth no one needs to be "guided" in the midst of their own guidance.

All guidance is always available to you and is already within you. In a certain sense, whereas you have the impression that you are just opening to guidance and that you are retrieving and finding guidance through growth, the truth is that being in physical incarnation has diminished your immediate access to the all knowing guidance of your Higher Self and All That Is. All you are truly doing is reestablishing your ability to communicate with your Higher Self and higher consciousness, a talent that will become much more readily available as you evolve to a higher vibrational state.

Unmasking Your Truth

Q: There is so much fear, apprehension and uncertainty in the world right now – the world situation is spiraling out of control, the economy continues to struggle, war has caused waves of refugees around the globe and major changes are happening to us everyday. In the midst of all this, many of us feel we have reached places in our careers, our relationships and in our lives where we feel overwhelming anxiety and personal dissatisfaction. What is going on and how does it relate to our personal journey?

The time when you are able to retreat or hide from yourself is quickly coming to a close. For if you cannot be truthful with yourself about who you are, then how can you survive and remain grounded in an environment where your sensitivity is enhanced, your senses are constantly bombarded, you are all seeing all the time and where you are open to a flood of universal energies bringing you new awareness and, in its path, heightened emotional trauma?

While avoiding or hiding your truest self might have been easy even a short time ago, when you were bathed and cushioned in a family, a small town, a village or other "tribal" associations and beliefs where you could believe what you were told to believe or pretend to be something not related to your true nature and your Truth, this is no longer possible. Why would this be so?

We have told you many times that most of you will be headed towards future incarnations in a world that provides you with genetic qualities that have Fifth Dimensional attributes. Among these attributes, you will find that certain forms of telepathy are a prized new sense, just as hearing, smell and touch are senses you know well in the Third Dimensional environment that you know. If this is so, you will participate in future lifetimes in a world where everyone understands everyone else's true nature. In such a world, it is not possible to hide your feelings or masquerade. Your truth becomes whom you are, visible for the entire world to see.

As the universal and Ascension energies in the world you now know intensify, so do the situations being experienced. As the Timeline of which you are part speeds up and approaches collapse, merging as part of the Ascension process with a new Timeline that will continue on for those destined to remain within incarnations in the Third Dimension, you experience a kind of "dress rehearsal" pertaining to the future traits you will have. To prepare you, your Higher Self purges you of those patterns and worn out masks that you have become so accustomed to wearing in front of each other. In many cases these masks have become so ingrained, you have forgotten which is true and which is false. In some cases the beliefs and ideas you hold that were forged around your families, your friends, your communities, your work and even your governments are so removed from your own current Truth that it is unrecognizable to you.

How is it possible then to rediscover one's "Truth?" What transpires in such a case is the disintegration around you of anything that is not related to that Truth. While we appreciate and understand that Truth is ever changing, just as you are beings that are ever changing, those many things that you have done to bend over backwards trying to accommodate your belief structure and make things "work out", trying as hard as you can to walk on eggs and play hide and seek with yourself endlessly, are no longer possible.

Thus, each of you is being triggered, through dissatisfaction or through obligation, to re-find your "Truth." You are being guided through chaos and dissatisfaction to eliminate what is no longer relevant and no longer True for you and, in a sense, re-identify and reinvent yourself for the world that ultimately is coming.

As you do so, there is massive upheaval and change all around you. In your personal lives, it is the reason you feel insecure, as you watch some lifelong friends, relationships and associations fall by the roadside. It is for this reason there is a new sense of inequality and injustice. It is even for this reason that there are currently mass exoduses, whether you are speaking of people migrating far and wide to escape violence, those forced to find new homes in the wake of disaster, those forced into new careers under the weight of changing business norms or those seeking new ways of existing in a world that seems newly unfamiliar.

It is also precisely for this reason that world economies and economic values are shaky, that organizations are experiencing scandal or taking bold new directions never seen before and that world governments are experiencing grid lock and failure to move forward. Although you find yourselves at the moment when these institutions continue to hold onto outmoded beliefs in an effort to maintain themselves, they find their very existence threatened by all kinds of groups of a lower vibrational resonance delivering mayhem and devastation to their doors that threaten the very fabric of their being. In a manner of speaking, chaos is not only at the gate, it has infiltrated your world structure in an effort to hasten its demise and, thus, force you to redefine and reinvest in your own Truth.

Such moments are perilous indeed, and vigilance must be maintained. Vigilance comes in the form of self-awareness and Truth, and realigning with your Truth, whatever that may be, ensures a higher resonance and stronger vibrational quality. This is your armor and this is your protection in such turbulent times. But in finding your Truth, beware of false prophets, organizations or those that would have you adhere to this or that dogma or doctrine. Truth is a personal experience that is defined only by an effort to raise your consciousness and remain integral to your Soul's path, without the need to enforce your Truth on anyone or anything else or the obligation to follow something that is not your Truth.

If you are not currently aligned with your Truth, if you are not aligned with your higher purpose -- your Essence Path -- and if you are not unified with the coming higher dimensional frequencies, your journey will be challenging, problematic at best. Simply stated, that which no longer holds Truth for you will not survive the intense influx of energies.

Only what is True for you, only what is real for you and only what is aligned with your higher purpose will survive the coming evolution. Remember that from chaos comes an obligation to renew your own Truth. In the midst of such turmoil, opportunities for growth abound and individuals, families, groups, organizations, communities and even nations that reestablished their Truth now (whether they are forced to or do so voluntarily) will emerge stronger and truer to their purpose than ever before. This is what you should strive for, and in doing so, you not only lighten your load and arm yourself, you become a beacon of higher consciousness and an example to all.

When Adversity Seems Relentless

Q: The challenges occurring now are confusing and relentless. There are times when I feel that the events taking place around us, whether they are political, societal or environmental, can no longer be avoided and are becoming insurmountable. What is happening to our world and why is this taking place?

At a time in the grand cycle of Ascension when you are faced with the obligation to discover who you are and align with your own inner truth, it is only natural that you are faced with events that force you to consider what in fact you believe and on what your inner Truth is actually based. During the course of such a time, things you face that immediately resonate as being false, even abhorrent and despicable, surface forcing you to examine your inner belief structure.

As this occurs, the things you consider to be deceitful and lacking Truth are louder, more devastating and more sensational than ever before. It is as if the Universe is forcing you to discover and reconfirm your Truth by witnessing through your heart the things you know to be wrong, false and evil.

Thus the period you are experiencing now is intended to bring each of you into close alignment with your own Truth, whatever that "Truth" for you might happen to be. In doing so, the Universe intends to push you towards thought patterns that are consistent with your Truth. When this happens, you are able to come into closer association with energetic patterns that will magnetize to you likeminded individuals so that ultimately, when you are congregated together, you will be positioned to attract into your reality events that match your vibrational resonance.

In this way, the mass conscious belief structure of those who are banded together with the same Truth will attract into reality events that are consistent with their level of Soul consciousness and Soul age. The widening disparity and separation of beliefs you see happening all around you is indicative of this. Thus the congregating of individuals who have similar Soul age, beliefs and life preferences becomes an important aspect of Ascension. As this process continues, you will see more and more extreme division, divisions that in time will seem to separate friends, families, businesses, whole communities and even nations as the current timeline continues to emerge.

We have said many times in the past that the belief structure you have – your Truth, if you prefer – creates a vibrational resonance that magnetizes reality and attracts to you, and others in your proximity, the events that become the fabric of your lives. It is not by accident that for many years now we have informed you that what you think and what you feel are universal acts that contribute to your vibrational resonance and attract a reality that is similar in vibration. If you will, your personal worldview, which often includes your family, friends, community, culture and even your nation, individually and jointly attract events that respond electromagnetically to whatever vibrational wave is being emitted. What you focus on, personally and en-mass, becomes vibrational intention, and this in turn attracts events and situations – we prefer to term them opportunities for growth – to you.

But this does not mean that you are subject to the many challenging events that transpire, unless of course you participate in the vibrational resonance of those events. Participation takes place through your beliefs, the thoughts you have based on your beliefs, the similarities in your patterns of thought and the emotional content (in particular fear) with which you imbue your beliefs. These elements combine to become the way you see the world - your "Truth."

An example is warranted. A young man takes a journey to a far off land. He meets amazing people and sees amazing new things. His belief that this journey will bring him wondrous and joyful things, or even his simple naivety and lack of preconceived notions about what will happen there, provides him with experiences that reinforce his belief that all is well and he is meeting amazing, accepting and joyful events. When he does come face to face with something that is not consistent with his belief system, he quickly turns from it, recoups his energy and chooses to take another route where once again he meets experiences consistent with his belief. His "Faith" (of the universal sort and not the religious type) is clearly being demonstrated in real terms through the physical reality that passes right in front of his eyes. Even surrounded or faced with challenging situations, people or events, they evaporate as he enters the scene – at least for him and from his perspective.

An older man sets out on the same journey. He believes that where he is going is poverty-stricken, the people are beggars and thieves, the language is incomprehensible and he will be ostracized for being an outsider. His vibrational resonance not only attracts the very things he believes but these are also the only things he sees since these are the glasses (of belief) through which he now sees the world. Needless to say, he is robbed, threatened, treated poorly by the natives and surrounded by a relentless torrent of uncomfortable events. His experiences confirm to him that his beliefs were right all along and this is truly a horrible place.

Finally, these two meet up and trade their impressions of the land they are visiting. The young man is mystified and appalled when he hears the older man's descriptions of places and things he has found magical, easy and joyful. To him the old man is senile and cranky, and the tales he tells are completely fabricated, false and untrue. The young man believes he is hearing fake news from the older man.

Similarly, the old man thinks the young man a fool. He is certain the youngster is crazy or on drugs, and the old man is convinced the young man will certainly be kidnapped by gangs, injured in a natural catastrophe and robbed by locals. To him, the young man has told him tales that are completely fabricated, false and untrue. His experience has told him otherwise so he is certain the young man is disseminating fake news.

Both the young man and the old man saw the Truth – their Truth -- as it appeared to them. Neither was better or worse, good or bad. Neither perspective was fake in the eye of the beholder. But clearly one Truth was a joyful experience and one was full of challenge and fear. Both however, were real, exemplified through the experiences of the person who navigated them. This example demonstrates that; 1) Your belief structure has significant impact on your resonance, which then attracts events of similar resonance; and 2) Each attracts experiences that align with their inner "Truth."

Although you tend to see the world in duality, with a right and wrong, good and bad side, as seen in our example, we would suggest that there is also a tertiary alignment that we have called neutrality or non-alignment. This is not to diminish the fact that certain sides of the duality might seem clearly wrong or even evil, but rather demonstrates that often those who come into direct conflict and opposition tend to be different sides of the same coin, vibrating at essentially the same resonance. While the details may vary greatly, as an example we would suggest that a Fundamentalist follower of one religion may be very similar to its counterpart who is a Fundamentalist follower of a different religion, despite the fact that they both profess to detest each other and have vowed to destroy one another at every turn.

It becomes clear then that it is not always a question of choosing sides or whether you should align yourself with this or that particular political group, cultural standard or religion, though such a choice might seem inevitable or even be demanded by your society. As we have said, it is likely that one or both sides appear right or wrong, good or evil. Remember that what you see as good or bad, right or wrong is based on your personal belief structure and is an indication of your vibrational resonance. That resonance is magnetic to the ethereal substance that creates real events and your physical reality.

But what is truly important here is the realization that you can no longer be silent in yourself about what you believe and what your own Truth actually is. Your Truth can no longer remain hidden to you by yourself or from others, as it often was in the past. You are being forced to align with your "Truth" and obliged to make an inner choice by seeing the depths of despair, disparity and depravity of whatever you consider to be NOT Truth, as it were.

Your Truth will no longer be silenced inside you, and the louder, more unacceptable and even despicable events that you focus on or confront become, the clearer it is that you are being guided to make a choice. Thankfully perhaps, the more you are NOT able to submerge the feelings you have associated with the events happening before your eyes the easier your choice of "Truth" actually becomes. But this is only the beginning of the process. Once you have found the appropriate alignment, your Truth becomes a vital component, via your vibrational resonance, of the elements that assist you to find similar vibration and consciousness in your world.

This ultimately leads you to the place where like-minded individuals and communities (to you) reside – in other words, you are prompted, through your Truth to find peace and harmony through the need to identify, locate and join with those who think, feel and act as you do. Once Truth has been established and aligned within you, anything that you deem untruth, whether it comes from your best friend, a neighbor, a hate group or even the President of your country, becomes so distasteful it repulses you, as well it should if you are to be true to yourself and your Soul.

It is incorrect however, to think that finding your Truth or making your choice requires your physical participation or interaction, and this is important to remember. You are not necessarily being guided to take to the streets with this or that cause (unless this is what you desire) or physically accomplish or do anything. Therein lies the beauty of your tertiary (energetic) choice (a Fifth Dimensional effect, as we have explained in "Timeline Collapse and Universal Ascension"). We would suggest that this third choice of non-alignment through the finding of one's Truth is emerging in those of higher consciousness at this time, and this leads them to align with their Truth while also seeking "higher ground" as it were.

This is because once you align with your inner Truth, you have taken the first step in changing your vibrational patterns so that you can begin to attract to yourself like-minded situations, consciousness and physical reality. As a result, together with like-minded individuals you are able to generate physical events and experiences in your life that are more compatible with your Soul's goals, not to mention better suited to a (usually) higher vibrational quality.

If you will, aligning with your Truth in this manner begins the process of attracting the very people, events and situations that will rescue you from the challenges and (potentially) deliver you from spiraling world events that are seemingly relentless and beyond your control. That is, of course, if this is your intention and the intention of your Soul. In this way, you rise, in terms of consciousness, above any conflict being fought by duality groups that have essentially the same lower vibrational frequency, whatever side they may appear to be on.

As we have said often in the past, Younger Souls are now proliferating on the Earth plane and these younger Souls will actually be those entities starting or continuing incarnations in a newly emerging time-space wave of Third Dimensional Reality. It is with this in mind that the challenges present and coming seen on the timeline of the Third Dimension will become more and more visible (louder and louder) to you as the timeline progresses. This is due to the fact that generally Younger Souls choose to progress in consciousness by experiencing sometimes dramatic external karmic situations. Older Souls prefer self-karmic lessons and introspection for Soul growth rather than outward participation in mass catastrophic events.

Older Souls of higher consciousness who wish to continue on peacefully in current lifetimes within such an emerging Third Dimensional Reality would do well to understand this and be clear about what is actually transpiring, from a higher perspective, in their world. This clarity, which tends to emerge as a result of the enormous stress experienced witnessing overwhelming en-masse events around you, actually serves as higher guidance coaxing you unconsciously into the need to find peace and safety. Such awareness acts energetically to protect and deliver you from the many conflicts and catastrophic events that will be occurring on the future timeline.

Proximity to these events becomes a guide to the nature of your own consciousness, and your distaste for the situations you see, as well as your desire to extract yourself from them, is potentially the greatest indication of where you stand in the process. Naturally, some Older Souls will participate deeply in these events for purposes of rapid Soul growth. However, we would suggest that the majority will find such situations disturbing and abhorrent and (making the tertiary choice) will choose to not align with the lower vibrational resonance that attracts the events in the first place. Older Souls will intuit guidance and make choices that allow them to disengage from individuals, communities, locations and societal structures where lower energies attract such challenging events. Younger Souls, those who inevitably prefer the rough and tumble karma of Third Dimensional events, will experience Soul growth through direct interaction and participation in the coming events, challenging or otherwise.

As we said, whether you find yourself in the midst of certain situations or are removed from them is almost always a result of where you hold your Truth and the resonating factors that attract reality to you. Ideally, Older Souls who have aligned with their Truth will recognize the need to find a place of inner peace and harmony where they feel comfortable and safe. Ultimately, this will lead them to search for, discover and congregate with individuals of higher consciousness who believe and think as they do, wherever those Souls may be.

This is not to suggest however, that Older Souls will be completely absent from the dramatic events happening, catastrophic or otherwise. Many will choose to participate for their own Soul or karmic purposes. But it is to say that in general, your immediate surroundings -- environmental, political and otherwise -- respond to the resonance of your Truth and the Truth of those in your proximity. That Truth is exponentially amplified in the creation of reality when it is unified energetically with those of similar resonance and thought patterns, wherever and whoever they may be. It is clear that for this reason, physically moving and leaving behind homes and locations that no longer align with your Truth is quickly becoming paramount to finding higher consciousness, safety, peace and harmony.

One needs look no further than the outpouring of love and assistance provided to victims of unnatural weather and catastrophic Earth events to understand that terrible situations generate mass Soul growth opportunities for all involved. However, there are those who would choose, through higher guidance and alignment with their Truth, to not be in close proximity to these disastrous events in the first place. Neither Soul choice (participating or not) is right or wrong, good or bad. Each choice has its purpose, and each is aligned with a particular Truth that either embroils you in the fray or delivers you prior to or during an impending disaster. (We will not for this discussion explore the nature and origins of the extreme Earth events happening now, which is another discussion completely – See "The Earth's Chakra System & "Un-Natural" Natural Disasters" in Chapter Two.)

It needs to be understood further that many of the leaders and individuals - political, military, cultural, business and other - that you think are for or against you are actually neither. In most cases, these entities are unconsciously fulfilling their own missions, creating and in many cases exasperating the events that you now find and may find in the future challenging. As the timeline progresses, however, and the events outlined in our book "Timeline Collapse and Universal Ascension" materialize, it will become clear how important it is to be aligned with your Truth so that inadvertently through fear, vibration and emotional input, you do not become overwhelmed and ultimately trapped in close proximity to the many challenging events, environmental and political, that will take place.

Seeing what your heart knows to be untrue forces you into alignment with your own inner Truth. And being in alignment with your Truth is precisely what will assist and guide you in the coming period. It will appear that many have been haphazardly thrown into the conflicts or accidentally find themselves in the midst of events beyond their control. Nothing could be further from the truth. Your proximity and participation in these events is almost always a factor of your personal karma, your Soul's desire, your fears, your Soul age, your vibrational resonance or a combination of all these things. How you traverse these events and whether you experience them from the inside or from afar will be based entirely on your Soul's goals, your belief structure, alignment with your personal Truth and the reality you are creating locally and regionally both individually and en-masse.

Many who are aligned with their Truth and who have been guided to extract themselves from situations that do not have their vibrational character, will likely find that they have been guided to places where, together with like-minded individuals, the events created locally are not as challenging or dramatic as they might otherwise be. For these individuals, dramatic en-masse events will still take place and potentially be witnessed by them, but will happen far off and at a safe distance. Their vibrational fortitude and "Faith" will still be tested however, and for these individuals it will become more important than ever before to banish fear and loathing in order to retain higher vibrational integrity and not attract to themselves the far off dramas they may witness.

But in order to find such a place of peace and harmony, many will be obliged to leave behind long time homes, families and friends. And though we do not wish to suggest that challenges of every sort will not be present in some form or another everywhere, we would state that the reward for finding Truth and following one's inner guidance is generally the ability to remain isolated and removed from the most devastating challenges your world faces. When harbored in places where the vibrational resonance is more stable and consistent with your own inner Truth, the events being generated and created in those areas tend to reflect the community's augmented vibrational state and consciousness, as well as the Soul's desires and the higher consciousness of the individuals involved in creating mass reality on a local basis.

Whatever your choice, let alignment with your own Truth, love of your fellow journey-men, association with the like-minded and a conscious desire for personal higher guidance be the hallmark of your experience. In this way you may rest relatively sure that for the most part, the personal reality that unfolds around you, taken within the context of the mass conscious reality being played as a backdrop to your lives, will be one that delivers you from conflict, devastation and dismay, whatever its origins may be.

As always, we wish you love and peace, and the ability to access the highest guidance as you discover and align with your personal Truth.

"Privacy, please!" How Truth & Privacy are Lessons in Respectfulness

Q: We hear a lot these days about data mining, personal privacy and the question of what is and is not "true." Almost daily we are told that our personal data is used to sway our inner-most thoughts and manipulate us, and we see concrete facts transformed into altered facts right before our eyes in an effort to convince or deceive us. Can you give us some insight into what is going on?

In order to provide you with a better understanding of the significance you face concerning the topics of Privacy and Truth, let us first take a brief look at certain relevant Ascension-related information we have discussed with you in the past.

First, it should be clear that as the current timeline progresses, a great many of the Souls now in physical incarnation in the Third Dimensional environment will cycle-off following their current incarnation. That is to say, many Souls have reached the point of maturity in terms of consciousness and are positioned to take advantage of the universal Ascension process happening during this important period.

As a result of their higher consciousness, these Souls will be able to raise their vibrational frequency in conjunction with the Ascension of the current Third Dimensional time-space wave. This will enable them to end the cycle of incarnations on Third Dimensional Earth and proceed to Fifth Dimensional incarnations on Earth's Fifth Dimensional counterpart, Terra. Naturally, this is the appropriate evolution for most Human Angelic Souls, and it is important to note that these Souls, who are poised to Ascend, have reached the level of consciousness and vibrational integrity that is needed to manage and properly adjust to Fifth Dimensional incarnations where expanded physical and sensory attributes are the norm.

Physical incarnations on Fifth Dimensional Terra are far different from the physical incarnations you currently know and experience on Third Dimensional Earth. While the expanded higher consciousness attributes vary in nature, as discussed in our recent book, "Timeline Collapse," perhaps the most interesting and distinctly new attribute you will possess and experience in a Fifth Dimensional environment is an augmented sense of perception -- intuitive knowing. Every Fifth Dimensional incarnate has naturally what you might term the gift of "inner sight", psychic and intuitive abilities, if you will, which, though rare, are increasing in your Third Dimensional realm.

The expanded Fifth Dimensional sensory attribute of intuition and inner knowing allows one to intuitively have the ability to know and clearly identify "Truth", distinguishing it from falsehood and even giving the perceiver an understanding of why this or that is, in fact, the "Truth." This intuitive sense further allows one to objectively and without judgment instantaneously reach into the very depths of an individual entity's psyche.

Such inner sight is not as intrusive or invasive as you imagine, since it is a talent that all in Fifth Dimensional reality possess and hold with great humility and understanding. Rather, it provides every entity the ability to not only "know" each individual's Truth, but also allows them to understand all aspects of another's Soul journey, including their life mission, their various experiences up to the point of encounter and a "behind-the-scenes" look at their personality traits, challenges and opportunities. Since this information is understood to be seen from the higher perspective of each individual's Soul, judgment or condemnation of any individual becomes mute, since the reason and substance of their personal journey is viewed as it relates to the higher growth of their Soul. Naturally, this inner-sight perception is reserved for older Souls that have reached a level of consciousness where, unlike many younger Souls found in Third Dimensional reality, there is no desire to judge or oblige anyone to conform to specific dogmas or any path that is not their own.

Such an understanding is far removed from the Third Dimensional duality model. Within the Third Dimensional reality, good and bad, right and wrong, heaven and hell are the only possible perspectives. Duality - as well as the need to choose one side or the other - battles endlessly within the psyche of baby and younger Souls. Fifth Dimensional reality on the other hand provides older Souls with a tertiary polarity - the polarity of complete neutrality. This objectivity, which fosters tolerance and the desire to live and let live is the normal standard of Fifth Dimensional incarnation.

Now, in a world where such inner knowing is prevalent, it becomes clear that Truth is easily recognized and discerned. Furthermore, Privacy, or what you perceive as Privacy, is not necessarily something sought since in knowing the Truth through inner sight, there is nothing left to hide. In fact a true inner knowledge of exactly what an individual has chosen as their life mission and work, and the reason for such choices, makes the notion of Privacy that you experience seem relatively quaint.

However, such an arrangement is only possible in a dimension where everyone has this same ability, and everyone, as it were, is an open book. This renders the use of such Truth for purposes of deceit, control or manipulation unproductive, if not unconscionable. In other words, if you were to inwardly know without question the "Truth," understand the deep seated reasons someone acted as they did, knew their impulses and what drove them in advance and realized who they were was related to their Soul's desired choices for personal growth in that lifetime, would you not be less judgmental and less concerned with trying to force someone to do things your way or to your advantage? Add to this the fact that they also know your Truth, and you see the futility of trying to falsify Truth or deceive someone about their own path.

Entities incarnated on Fifth Dimensional Terra, who are only able to incarnate in such a frequency when they have mastered the need to manipulate, harm or force others to their way of thinking, something younger Souls often do, understand what a gift this particular sense provides. Fifth Dimensional beings are focused on their own personal growth through the understanding of their inner nature and are not at all concerned with the need to manipulate or change others. Manipulating others through clandestine efforts is neither desired nor possible since such manipulation would be readily known. Therefore, Privacy is not an issue.

But this is NOT the case in Third Dimensional reality. In the Third Universal Dimension, where younger Souls predominate and are increasing incarnations at this time, the arrangement through technology of knowing the inner personal workings of various groups of individuals by those who are intent on controlling and manipulating the individuals they have secretly gathered that inner knowledge from, is an affront to the sanctity of the individual and violates higher universal law.

We have told you that many currently incarnating in the Third Universal Dimension will soon be Ascending to incarnations in the Fifth Dimension. Furthermore, you should know by now that the current Third Dimensional reality is in the process of Ascending to Fifth Dimensional frequency, just as the Second Dimension will soon evolve into a new Third Dimensional timeline. As we have also mentioned, there are those Souls (mostly baby and younger Human Angelic Souls) who will continue on in the newly emerging Third Dimensional timeline. These younger Souls will repopulate the new Third Dimension as older Souls cycle off and establish new incarnations at higher dimensional frequencies.

At this moment then, you have entities that are incarnated in lifetimes on a Third Dimensional timeline of Earth living side-by-side with those entities that will soon be cycling off to Fifth Dimensional incarnations on Terra. Such a transition is gradual in nature and almost unperceivable to those of lower consciousness. One needs look no further than to the emergence worldwide of diametrically opposed groups that seem to become more entrenched in ideology and the consequential separation it fosters every day.

In many cases, these groups begin to form and utilize their own view of reality, and when looked at they appear to be living in an alternate

Universe or at the least, living according to alternative facts. We would suggest that this is indicative of the current Ascension phenomena we are discussing, where these individuals are in fact reshaping their personal reality to meet their goals and needs. We would further tell you that until such time as the Ascension process has completed over approximately the coming 250 years these divisions should become more and more pronounced.

It is because of this that we have spoken often about the importance, now more than ever, of finding one's Truth. Truth, and what is true, comes to the forefront at this time in order to force your consideration and provoke you to seek your Truth. In doing so, the process allows you to align with the reality that is most akin to your Soul and your wellbeing.

But what is paramount to understand is that seeking the Truth is not necessarily a debate of what the Truth actually is. Rather, it is your obligation to seek and find YOUR Truth. The nature of the current division not only demands that younger Souls find each other, it requires that older, more enlightened Souls also do the same. Finding your Truth, the Truth that resonates with you, is what will bring you to those of like mind. Together, you will generate a mass conscious reality that is derived from your "Truths", and in doing so, hopefully, you will be guided to a more enlightened environment and insulated from the coming turmoil.

Bear in mind that reality is constructed based on your personal belief structure -- your Truth. That means it is based on what you believe to be true, NOT what the actual Truth might happen to be, since many Truths and many converging realities are possible. Knowing this, you realize that what the Truth actually happens to be is a debate you will soon tire of, finding it as endless as it is pointless to convince someone of a Truth that is not their own.

It is quite possible for there to literally be many different mass conscious realities generated concurrently around varying belief systems within the same time-space. Where you place your Truth (belief) then have much to do with the reality magnetized to you. Additionally, the nature of the Truth, and subsequently the reality that is drawn to you, is not only an indication of your Soul age and consciousness, it also places you in alignment with your Soul's intention -- your Essence Path. In a way, finding your Truth becomes a precursor to creating and understanding your own personal reality, something you will begin to realize more and more as this timeline progresses.

Returning to the issue of Privacy then, as the question of Truth emerges it also exposes considerations concerning Privacy. If Truth exists in relationship to the consciousness of the entity experiencing it and is also the precursor of a belief structure that creates personal reality, protecting and respecting that inner process becomes important. If left unguarded, it is an Insight into one's inner world that can be exploited or disrespected by those of lower consciousness and devious intent. The consideration of respect for an individual's inner world, through Privacy, also provides a means of identifying who exactly possesses a neutral, objective and more mature consciousness from those with a lower consciousness who would seek to use the inner knowledge of someone's Truth for their own purposes, among which greed and the desire to control you figure prominently.

So here you are witnessing a time when polarizing separations of Truth, spurred by vastly contrasting levels of consciousness, ultimately lead you to conversations around protecting the inner and personal information (Truth) of each individual. Some among you begin to feel mindful of the information gathered from others through technological advancement and acknowledge the Privacy that ability now necessitates. Those of a decidedly more tribal orientation (younger Souls who believe the world should only be stocked with "Me" and other "Me's") ignore the need to protect each individual's inner Truth. Instead they look to either force an individual to their way of thinking, or seek to benefit from the stolen knowledge to control or manipulate an individual or the population.

We assure you that such self-service motivations of power, control and greed are in this case more closely aligned with lower Third Dimensional karmic consciousness than with a higher Fifth Dimensional vibration. Your personal information is not being used in such instances for the greater good, as you may be told by those who gather it, but instead is being used by planetary (as well as off-planetary) groups who seek to dominate you, possibly with the intent to even usurp the planetary Ascension process.

So what exactly is happening in a world where technology permits you to unlock the veil and look at the inner world of an individual? The answer is two fold. First of all, entities who are growing in consciousness and will ultimately Ascend to higher Fifth Dimensional lifetimes are, without realizing it, "practicing" as they experience what it is like for others to have the ability to see and "know" the inner workings of every individual. If you will, this is a primitive version of the experience you will have with Fifth Dimensional awareness where others will innately have inner sight and will be aware of your most personal inner Truth. Again, recall that such telepathy is an innate sense possessed by every being incarnated in the Fifth Universal Dimension.

It is not by accident that issues surrounding Truth - what is true and what is not -- have come up in your world first, followed now closely by issues around Privacy and the need to find and protect one's inner Truth/information. For many, the issue of Truth and Privacy appear to be completely unrelated, but in fact they are different aspects of the same valuable lesson of respect and empathy.

As your experience around Truth becomes practical, and as the "Truth" of each individual is brought to light and revealed, each of you comes to realize the importance of respecting your Truth. Those who state proudly that they have been "true to themselves" do so with good reason. Once this is mastered, next you become aware of the intrinsic value of everyone's personal inner information, which, in enlightened individuals, naturally leads to a desire to safeguard Truth through the protection of private information.

Finding Truth becomes a lesson in self-respect. Self-respect leads to the consideration of Privacy and provides a lesson in protecting and respecting the inner Truth of every individual.

Secondarily, it is for this reason that individuals from older Soul groups have now come together in an attempt to protect the sanctity of their inner knowledge -- their Truth. This is the case in various parts of the world, such as in the European Union, where older Souls, mindful of Privacy, coordinate initiatives whereby an individual is respected and protected. The inner Truth of each person, obtained through technological advancement, is to be respected by being placed out of the reach of lower consciousness entities that would otherwise exploit it through secrecy and deceit. Countries and societies that lag in doing so demonstrate their domination by younger Souls and lower consciousness entities that would rather hold onto and linger in lower dimensional vibration.

As we have said, your world is experiencing an exodus in terms of those Souls who are departing lifetimes within the current realm and who are destined, through Ascension, for lifetimes in higher vibrational Universes. Those Souls are readily being replaced by a myriad of baby and younger Souls that do not necessarily have the level of consciousness needed to understand the importance of Truth or, as a result, the need to respect personal Privacy. For the most part, the entities destined to continue on within incarnations in the Third Dimension, where Soul growth is primarily obtained through karmic interaction, have no need or desire to curtail access to their private inner worlds, since in many cases the rape of their Truth serves as the fuel of their karmic endeavors and future growth.

This is not so for individuals who have reached a higher level of consciousness. In that respect, if the world you see emerging before you is one that seems alien to your nature and distasteful to you, difficult though it may be living in such a reality, congratulate yourself nonetheless on knowing that you feel this way because the reality you are seeing does not align with your Truth. Nevertheless, continue to seek out your Truth, work to find like-minded individuals and insulate your reality from outside forces carrying their beliefs like torches that are alien and unsavory to you. Remember that while it is not always evident to you, doing so ensures a personal reality generated based on your own Truth and this is your best defense in a wayward world. Your Truth and the beliefs it generates will ultimately shield you from external tampering, and insulate your experiences no mater what version of mass conscious reality appears to be raging all around you.

It is not for us to tell you upon which side you should place your allegiance. Instead, we simply wish you to be informed about the higher, often hidden reason these things occur in your world. As we have said already, understand that your inner and intuitive reaction to these things is in fact a good indicator of your level of consciousness, your Soul age, your growth and perhaps even your ability to move forward through the evolutionary process of Ascension in the coming period.

For those of you who are beginning to understand the nature of their personal "Truth", who are beginning to align themselves with that Truth and who are understanding the need to be respectful of Privacy and the personal information of each individual, we wish you well as you continue to seek your Truth. Remember to be impartial, objective and clear headed in your search for Truth, and be respectful of yourselves and others you meet on your journey. In doing so, may you create a world reality that resonates for you, where acceptance, love, respect and protection of the inner workings of every Human Angelic Soul are guaranteed.

Chapter 5
The Creation of Physical Reality

Conscious Intention

We have in the past discussed with you that this current period is an important period in the time known to you as Ascension. This transition period is the time that truly separates the adults from the children in terms of Soul age and Soul energy for it is the time when you will discover your true purpose and your power in the world. But what perhaps is more important is that the current energies coming into your realm are related to this transitional period and, as we have said, related to the transition from Third to Fifth Dimension in a simultaneous occurrence that allows you to live side by side with those who will remain in Third Dimensional incarnations in the future and those who will rise vibrationally and, ultimately, physically to incarnate in Fifth Dimensional lifetimes. Until such time as you incarnate in a truly Fifth Dimensional environment, where Earth is known as "Terra," you will continue to live alongside those within the Third Dimensional realm that you currently know.

But there are important distinguishing factors regarding this of which you must become aware. And you must become aware of these factors for they will become more and more intense and more and more important as time goes on. As the energies increase, those with certain vibrational qualities will find that easily and quickly what is thought will materialize into physical reality. This is the reason that we have discussed with you prior that it is so vitally important to be aware and to be conscious of your thoughts. As we have said, thoughts are actions. And now, more than ever before, what you think shall in fact be made manifest in your lives without the delays of the past and in relatively short time.

In order to help you focus and understand the true meaning and impact of this, we wish to discuss with you a principle and a process that we shall term "Conscious Intention ™". It is your intention made conscious or rather your conscious intention that allows you to control what it is that you are creating in your life. In the past, you were like ships tossed about on waves. What you thought was created willy-nilly, sometimes created here, sometimes created there, sometimes never made manifest. Your manifestation of reality, of physical reality, the events and actual things that happened to you in your lives were random in nature because, to a greater or lesser degree, they were unconsciously manifest. It was in this sense that your innermost fears were created and delivered willy-nilly to you, and it was in this manner that you grew and learned responsibility of your creative nature and reached an understanding, ultimately, of your true power.

Now we move into a new phase in the story of Third Dimensional creation. No longer will what you believe, think or fear be unconsciously or randomly created. Now what you believe, think and feel consciously will allow you to focus energy in such a way that manifestation of what you are consciously intent on creating will not only be possible, but will be almost immediately rendered in your life.

We have in the past briefly described the physical act of creation – the act of drawing reality and its events to you. We will again provide you with a basic understanding.

Your emotional content, the feelings that so many of you banish to the realm of hokum, are actually reflective of your belief structure and your innermost desires. Those feelings and emotions are heartfelt and are heart centered. They rise from the heart chakra and their true purpose is to communicate to the brain a certain frequency and wavelength and, in that respect, the brain along with the DNA at a cellular level are antenna waiting to pick up the impulses received from the emotions from the heart. When the brain, or your mental body, receives the messaging of emotion (which again is based on your beliefs both conscious and subconscious,) it then signals further to each and every cell within the body a certain vibrational and energetic state that it demands be created. As the cellular structure changes and vibrates in resonance with the brain's signaling, which in turn is receiving its messages from the heart; your cellular structure is then poised to communicate with the atoms and molecules in your reality. These are then reformulated so that they create (invite is perhaps the best term) the events, the situations, the people, the things and the places that become your reality and your life.

Now, more than ever before, this relationship can be measured. And it is for that reason that conscious intention becomes so vitally important. You have within you the awakening, and thus the power, to understand the basis of your emotions and feelings, and this allows you to master and control them rather than be mastered or controlled by them. By using your awakened consciousness, your conscious ability to focus attention and energy, you are able to interpret your feelings and your emotions and, where necessary, change them so that the signals being received by your brain, and thusly those sent to your cellular structure, are also altered. In this way, the reality in which you live is able to change as well, since reality will almost always acquiesce to your cellular vibration and your demand.

This is the principle of Conscious Intention. And it must be understood that whereas in the past you thought about things with intent only occasionally from time to time, spending perhaps 5% of your time in conscious mindfulness, while spending the rest of your time lost in trance, creating life in a willy-nilly and mostly subconscious manner, now the table may be turned. The more mindfulness and conscious intention you have, the more your reality will reflect that conscious intention. Now you must recognize and be aware that every waking moment of consciousness is a moment when you can control your feelings and your intention. By doing so, because of the extraordinary energies your world is being bathed in currently, you have the power to manifest your intention almost immediately into reality. Using the principle of Conscious Intention, now you have the power to manifest health and wellbeing. Now you have the power to manifest happiness. Now you have the power to manifest prosperity and joy at all times of day, at all times of the month and throughout the year. Through Conscious Intention, you become deliberate co-creators, no longer subject to the willy-nilly subconscious attraction of affairs reflected in past creations of reality.

Through the understanding that you must consciously be aware from moment to moment how you feel, what you are experiencing in terms of your emotion and what you are thinking, you gain access to the principles of reality's manifestation. Knowing that what is in your heart is always projected to your mental body, your mind, and that what is in your mind is then communicated to your DNA and entire cellular structure is the key to understanding that your resonance and vibratory frequency is at the essence of what attracts certain similar thoughts and situations into your life.

This becomes important because, as we have said, now more than ever before, the intensity of the energies present within your world will manifest reality quite readily and quite quickly right before your eyes. We do not intend to suggest that you will be able to "conjure" reality out of the blue, for Third Dimensional physics continue to apply, but we do wish to suggest to you that you will have the power to bring forth and create similar vibrational frequencies in the form of events, situations and people, in almost an uncanny and unprecedented manner.

And in this you must understand that while your higher self has compassion and unconditional love of you, it is your cellular structure that obeys your every command. If the feelings and emotions emanating from your heart are fearful, are subconscious, are disharmonic, are worried or are in any way negatively charged, that is what you will be communicating to your mind and mental body, and that is what you will be instructing your cellular structure to attract to you in the reality at large. Now is the time when you are being coaxed to not only master your emotional expression but to actually take control of that which you create. Now is the time to consciously banish all fear, anger, hate, discontent, envy and greed as well as all feelings and any emotional content that originates within you that is not in keeping with who and what you wish to be.

Be gentle with yourselves in taking the steps towards constant Conscious Intention, but be vigilant too. Understand that this is not a process that happens overnight, but in fact a process of awakening, an important evolution in terms of personal transcendence and spiritual Ascension. Work at becoming consciously intent by being attentive, mindful and aware of how you feel and what you are communicating to yourself and to the world. Work diligently at becoming consciously aware moment to moment, aware of your feelings, your emotions and your beliefs. Let your results be your guide, and if there are blocks either within your physical being or in the events that are transpiring around you, seek out the cause within your heart and ask yourself why you are seeing the results that you do. Becoming consciously intent, living your life with Conscious Intention, will allow you to transcend this time period and will allow you to navigate the transformative period that is coming and is, in many ways already here. It will allow you to push away from the Third Dimensional reality beginning the process of understanding the nature of Fifth Dimensional existence in preparation for the time of Ascension.

The Power of Creation

We have told you in the past that what you resist in life will persist, but what you embrace and walk through will in fact disappear from your vision. Each of you knows well by now that you are the co-creators of your existence. What you fear is created. Similarly, what you love is created. Sometimes these are distinct and different. Sometimes, they are confused and unified. Understanding the differences and subtle links between the emotional outputs of energy that act as a vortex of energetic and physical magnetism is important to understanding what you create as well as the power of your creation.

What is perhaps not as easily understood is the fact that often what you become obsessed with and focus on incessantly is in fact related to a lesson you have chosen to work on, consciously or unconsciously, as essentially a "spiritual" being experiencing a "physical" encounter. When you are constantly faced with situations that seem to be beyond your control, you should know that more than likely this is in fact the case. Likewise, when you experience specific issues that, to you, have impact and depth, you are in fact doing so as a matter of conscious awareness. Things that befall you are never accidental or haphazard. But if you refuse to take notice or pretend that the things that are happening to you are beyond your control, you essentially provide these things with the control you have abdicated. When you understand that what is being attracted to you is necessitated as a matter of your conscious growth, it is then possible to step back and understand what is happening to you.

We have told you many times in the past that within the plane of duality where you currently find yourself incarnated, you have the option of experiencing life from either the positive or from the negative polarity of experience. Most will revolve through these polarities, experiencing some things from the positive pole and others from the negative pole. There is no right or wrong experience, and your Higher Self is unconcerned from which polarity you orchestrate your experience. It knows only that you have come to conscious awareness in order to experience certain physical realities as a matter of consciousness growth. All things can be learned from either pole, although it becomes clear that becoming conscious of this and experiencing life through the positive polarity is far less challenging than experiencing events from the negative pole.

Generally, your focus on particular issues, persons, places or things will merely recreate them over and over again in various formats. If you are experiencing life from the negative polarity, then essentially you will be dealing with these things as the same "demons," so to speak, although each encounter may seem to be completely new and unfamiliar to you. It is for this reason that we tell you that what you resist will in fact persist, recreating again and again.

On the other hand, what you become conscious of and embrace, negative or positive, will allow you the space to move beyond a particular lesson or event. How is that accomplished? It is accomplished through Faith. Not the Faith you know as the religious variety, but the variety that provides you with belief in yourself, your Higher Self and the Universe, and the assurance that what happens to you has hidden within it reasons that reason does not know.

Faith is accomplished through believing that what is transpiring is not accidental, has merit of some kind and is certainly not beyond your control. It is accomplished through unconditional love towards yourself and others providing you with the steppingstones of grace that ultimately allow you to walk through any situation blocking you, any person that you feel has wronged you or anything pushing to keep you silenced and minimized.

Believe that you are a miraculous Being. Believe that life is within your ability and your control, and life shall become everything you wish for. But if you choose to believe that others are responsible for your environment, or others and the situations being generated are conspiring against you or have the ability to oblige you to their will, you shall never be able to understand your real power. In refusing to acknowledge the power of your creation or become conscious of the events being attracted to you, in giving your power over to the individuals and situations that appear and reappear (in different forms) again and again, you are in fact subjecting yourself to re-experience the same demons over and over throughout the lifetime.

The Expression of Your Will

In the past we have spoken to you of conscious intention, and we have explained that every thought is an action and same or similar thoughts linked together become creative acts put into motion. When combined with your emotional state and level of consciousness, after being filtered through your pre-life karmic goals and your life mission, the vibrational resonance generated at a cellular level is a divine combination that ultimately attracts your personal reality.

What we perhaps may not have explained amply is that your heart serves as the focal point of your creative experience. As a multi-dimensional Being, you receive energetic messages via your heart. Your heart then communicates this to the mind/brain (your mental body) and the endocrine system where it is processed. These systems then raise or diminish your personal cellular response via a vibrational resonance created as a result of the emotional "grade" you have given the message received from your heart. That vibrational resonance, which is a vibrational signature of sorts, is not only transmitted to and translated unconsciously by the world around you, it becomes the principal electromagnetic element pushed forth by you into the world that inspires, attracts, magnetizes and draws into your proximity the reality that ultimately becomes your experience.

In this way and in a manner of speaking, the world can be said to be an approximate facsimile of where you place your vibrational focus. Your reality will always tend to align with the vibrational resonance that you, against the backdrop of mass consciousness, generate, whether what is being experienced is to your liking or not.

It is not by accident therefore, that the heart and one's emotional state are highlighted, romanticized and seen throughout esoteric and metaphysical literature as perhaps the most important center of the physical and energetic body. Nor is it by accident that unconditional love, which neutralizes the heart center freeing it from fear and negative output, is the basis of much spiritual training. Additionally, it is not incidental that mastering one's emotional state is a paramount principle of mindfulness, or that most meditative training or bio feedback techniques focus on grounding, centering and calming the heart center, using this center to calm the mind and focus the distribution of higher thought and energy to other chakras and energetic portals.

What has been forgotten in this mix is the concept of Free Will. Your Will, that is the ability to consciously focus the energy that is provided to you from your Higher-Self in the manner in which you choose, is a prime component of conscious intention. In this way, your Will can be said to be a precursor of conscious intention, or even that conscious intention is an extension of your Free Will.

Without your Will, you are cast out on an ocean of happenings randomly experienced. When however, you are the Master of your Will, you in fact direct your energy according to your conscious desire or intent. When this energetic flow unites however, you have the power to alter the very nature of your vibrational resonance, allowing the process of creation to follow your lead more closely.

We are discussing this because it has become apparent in your world that the concept of your Will is being relegated to an inferior position in the creation of reality. Many have lost hope, stifled feelings or been told that their Will is unimportant or extraneous to the creation of their desired reality. Many others have been trained into submission by a system or by a group that relegates one's own desires to the closet, preferring the dogma and rule of the majority or the wishes of the many. This is expressed in such old adages as "All for one, and one for All," which on the surface is pleasant enough sounding and sometimes necessary, but in reality serves to make each of you subservient to the Will of the group authority or greater majority.

This is particularly important at this time, where it is clear that there is an emergence of a struggle between younger Souls, those destined to remain incarnated in the Third Dimension, and older Souls who are transitioning and will eventually find their next incarnations to be Fifth Dimensional in nature. It may be helpful to recall that young Souls see the world as "Me, and other Me's." Their Will is turned over to the group mind. Older Souls, on the other hand, see the world as "Me, and others who are independent and separate from Me, each with their own life mission." The Will for an older Soul is the linchpin of creative expression and the key to a personalized reality, demonized though it might be by younger Souls and group authorities. (Bear in mind that older Souls generally have passed the need for outward karmic endeavor, and thus tend to be less aggressive or violent by nature as well as more compassionate and caring towards their fellow humans.)

As this separation in Soul age becomes more pronounced, one of the primary struggles will be centered on issues concerning the Will/Rights of the individual versus the Will/Rights of the masses. In fact, as always we would suggest that the situations, scenarios and arguments you see surfacing in the world around you are not by happenstance. We would further state that many of the contentious issues under debate publicly (some of which sound inane or silly to those of higher consciousness) serve the purpose of creating opportunities for reflection and growth of consciousness, allowing for greater lessons to be learned from both sides of the equation.

What those lessons are depends upon your specific vibrational resonance, your life mission and your own particular Soul age. Clearly though, younger Souls or those remaining in a Third Dimensional vibration will see things quite differently than those elevating their consciousness in preparation for new incarnations in fifth density in the future. Our point here, however, is that, as an example, debates concerning which bathroom "will" be used by what segment of the populace should perhaps be seen as a beard covering the true debate, which we suggest is based on lessons concerning the expression of Will in your lives as reflected in your society.

There are many reasons such debates are timely. The most prevalent, as we have mentioned, is vibrational and consciousness growth around group-Will versus individual-Will. This becomes important in a society and prevailing world culture where in the past, to a greater or lesser degree, the Will of the many has so often been superimposed on the Will of the few. Moreover, in a time where consciousness and vibrational resonance is opening up for so many Human Angelics, it is interesting that a seemingly inane debate about bathroom permission becomes ground zero and precursor to any discussion within your dimension as to who exactly has the authority and power to subjugate whom.

Clearly, there are those in positions of authority and power who would prefer that you not have a clear route to expressing your individual Will, for you are easier to manage as a population and a mass consciousness if your reality is haphazard and devoid of your own conscious intent. Whole religious dogmas are devoted to such an effort. If you are without Will, then your intention is not able to position itself in the attraction of your reality. In this way, you are easily placed into a state of fear as you become hypnotized by the drama of what is happening, by the news and events of the day or even by the local celebrity and social chatter around the issues; all of which hinders you from focusing on Truth. Make no mistake, however; the intention of such distractions, pointless banter and endless debate is an effort to derail your own individual Will.

Without Will, the conscious focus needed to change the probable course of your reality, which includes the events that transpire in mass consciousness and the world, is altered. Reality is then haphazardly delivered to you. When this occurs, you become an individual who must scramble to deal with whatever is thrown at you at whatever time, and in some cases, your life becomes a constant series of reactionary or defensive events.

However, if you are a master of your own Will, if you take that Will, that conscious desire you intended, and focus it through your thoughts and your actions, you become the purveyor and creator of the events that transpire in your world. Discounting for a moment karmic and pre-life contracts you have, this places your vibrational resonance within grasp. Not only is this true in terms of creating the events in reality that are external to you, such as those within the mass consciousness backdrop, but those events that take place in your personal reality as well.

Why is Will important? Because it becomes the main consideration in terms of determining the kind of world and environment you choose to participate in and of which you are part. If you are content, as many younger Souls might be, to have reality thrown at you, and as a result be forced to react and defend yourself constantly, then know at least that your Will is being suppressed and diminished. However, if as an older Soul you are of a higher conscious resonance -- if you are connected to the enlightenment of higher wisdom and guidance -- you become privy to your own inner consciousness. It is only in this manner that you will clearly see how the events upon which you focus are directly related to where you are on the road of mastering your Will.

Use Will wisely as the gift it is, and place it as a precursor to the choices you make. Rather than relegate it to the back seat in favor of any group commitment or dictate, harmonize it with the messages coming from your heart, trust your feelings and check your emotional state. Then accept it as a component of your conscious intention.

Always remember to frequently verify the validity of your choices since these are subject to change by constantly checking the caliber and quality of your thoughts. Be vigilant and mindful about the management of your thoughts as well as the emotions and emotional state they evoke. Through conscious awareness, work to not harm the spirit or suppress the Will of others. Do so unless their Will is being imposed upon you forcibly, in which case, you are being guided to remember your Truth and reminded by your Higher Self to preserve the integrity of your own Will. Recognize the subtle difference between the proper expression of your Will and an effort to exact control over others.

In this way you become the central player in your life, and you relinquish the need to remain in an endless state of reaction and control, destined to dance only as you are forced to dance. To master your dimensional reality, understand the value of your Will and focus it through your intention, your emotions, your desires and your thoughts. When this is achieved, you also master the understanding of conscious control of the energy that is ultimately you.

Once that is accomplished and you perfect your own participation in the Third Dimensional reality of Earth (regardless of whether or not the Third Dimensional reality around you ever reaches your idea of perfection), you become poised for the new experiences that await you in higher dimensional realities. It is within those higher dimensional realities that creation is closely linked to your individual Will, your intention and your thoughts. In such a reality, these things unify with greater accuracy and speed to magnetize the particles of creation (reality) to you in ways you are not fully accustomed to presently. Having mastered the proper expression of your Will, you are ready to exist in dimensions where reality -- and its consequences -- are manifest almost immediately, and, in some cases, instantaneously.

We bring each of you much love and peace – offered to you as an expression of our Will.

The Power of Words, Thought Control and the Altering of Physical Reality

We have often said that thought is action. The reason for this is that what you think, and the thoughts that are expressed and then felt by you create an electromagnetic vibration, a frequency if you prefer. This vibration has magnetic qualities, and it projects into physical reality and attracts similar frequencies and vibration. The more intense the feeling or emotion with which you imbue the thought, the more likely it is that events, people, situations and realities that are of a similar vibration will be attracted to you and literally show up in your life. This is the universal law of attraction.

This law is the fundamental principle of how your reality is created and magnetized to you. Patterns that resonate with your vibrational input and intent, positive or negative, materialize in your physical reality.

Add to this the fact that you are also predisposed to "see" the world in one-way or another. The way you "see" your world and what happens to you is related to the life mission your Soul chooses prior to the lifetime as well as a myriad of life personality features you also choose that are formed in childhood through your environment and surroundings. This combination colors the way your thought process occurs (often an unconscious occurrence) and this vibrational projection then attracts to you optimum lessons designed for specific goals related to your personal Soul growth. Understand this and you begin to understand how "thought" plus "emotional intent" plus "individual predisposition" forms the basis of how you attract your reality and the lessons that befall you.

What we have not discussed in depth in the past, however, is the importance of sound and the spoken word in the creation of your physical environment. Most of you know that sound is a frequency and a vibration but few understand its importance in creating reality. There are many references to this in religious and esoteric literature. In fact, it is sound, the power of sound and the frequency of sound that prompts the many teachings around the power of the spoken word.

Thus, the "Word" is referenced as an act of God, and in fact when a word is spoken, or a combination of sounds is created, it generates a form of sacred geometry that makes certain combinations of sound more poignant and powerful than many realize. In fact, the vibrational patterns and sacred geometry formed by sounds -- or the combination of letters in words and words in sentences that comprise language -- generates a vibrational pattern that can influence the very creation of physical reality. Have you never wondered why chanting, vocal prayer, drumming, singing and the like have such power to move you or even to miraculously heal?

In conjunction with this let's also take a moment to discuss the effect of sound vibration and frequency on mass consciousness. While each of you has specific and varied traits related to your personalities that affect the way in which you see the world and influence the elements attracted into your reality, this is also the case with mass consciousness. Group vibrational projections have enormous power to create the mass conscious environment and it is against the backdrop of that environment that many, if not all individual desires and events are actually incorporated into one's life and played out in the reality you experience.

Returning to our original discussion concerning sound and the spoken word, it is not by accident that in the English language, as an example, the word "spelling" has two meanings: one is related to the correct ordering of letters to create the sound of that word and an additional meaning is related to the conjuring of a magical experience - a Spell. And if you permit us to take this further, can it be an accident that the definition of a "Spell" is to cast a magical intention that creates a new physical reality? Moreover, have you ever wondered where the belief originated (fantastic as it may seem) that a certain compilation of words, sound and vibration, like Abracadabra, when spoken in a certain way, at a certain time, with a certain intent and emotion could actually have the power to alter current reality?

In other words, someone who employs the casting of "Spells" uses words and certain phrases to create a specific vibrational frequency intended to propel that which is desired into physical reality. While much of this is now relegated to the world of fantasy or, for some taught specific dogmas, the world of evil concoction, this practice is actually based on a fundamental precept of physical reality creation. That is, actual reality is propagated through the concentration of frequency, emotional intent and (sound) vibration in such a way as to order the attraction of particles and pull them into formation to create the world you see and the opportunities you experience.

We are addressing this issue with you today because many are currently being swayed by the vibrational sensations being experienced around them, and, perhaps more problematically, are being drawn into challenges related to the mass conscious reality that is emerging. Without realizing or being conscious of it, you are becoming prone to manipulation by words and speech -- sound -- being used to generate a vibrational frequency that creates a mass consciousness that is, more often than not, removed from your liking. In short, there are those around you, many in places of authority, that are casting a "spell" upon you through the repetitive use of sound, vibration and frequency and in doing so they are altering your reality.

For some, this vibrational manipulation is precisely what they wish to hear and for their own purposes of Soul growth, they are more than willing to be subjugated by the vibrational manipulation. For others, particularly those older Souls still present at this moment in your world, the degeneration and deterioration of the mass consciousness that they see is confusing at best and infuriating at worst.

An inability to understand that this manipulation is being cast upon you through the constant use of frequency and vibration found in the compilation of certain words, phrases and thought patterns allows the originator of those errant vibrational frequencies to garner the power to alter your physical reality. At the present moment, the objective has been mostly to generate fear, one of the most potent emotions for creating reality, within a population that is unaware of the manipulation it is experiencing. However, at a future moment not far on the emerging timeline, those understanding these creation principles will attempt to use technologically advanced frequencies to sway your individual thought patterns and push certain agendas into reality.

You see the basis of this emerging in the current debates around the infiltration of your media, social and otherwise, and efforts to externally manipulate your various life decisions. But you have not yet experienced the more severe strategies being created by several world governments based on technologies developed through contractual arrangements and in cooperation with inter-dimensional extraterrestrials. These thought fence and thought control technologies are being prepared for potential use and are intended to reach beyond your conscious awareness so that via vibrational frequencies your Soul's free will is curtailed.

By manipulating your inner most thought patterns before they emerge and directing your emotional output, these technologies are intended to direct the creation of physical reality in a specific manner favorable to those controlling the technology. This is a violation of universal law, which is well known to the cooperating extraterrestrials but not known to the participating secret Earth government organizations. Use of these technologies will ultimately trigger karmic intervention from higher dimensional guardians of the Human Angelic Soul group.

To return to the subject at hand however, whether digitally, virtually or audibly expressed, the proliferation of modern communication vehicles and technology for disseminating vibrational and emotional expression has become part of your world now for specific reasons. Primary among these is to awaken all individuals to their power as co-creators of reality and the need to strengthen your core belief structure. As you awaken to this understanding, if only through sheer disgust, you gain valuable insight into your ability to control the manipulation being forced upon you by those using their positions to broadcast a vibration of words, sounds and thoughts intended to transform your reality.

It is easy to fall into this vibrational trap and be subjugated through the very real hypnotic frequency and effects of sounds and words used in a relentless and repetitive fashion to invade the consciousness. Moreover, on a larger scale, this same hypnotic frequency has the power to alter mass consciousness generally, thus changing the existing physical reality, including events, challenging and otherwise, that are emerging on the current timeline. Whether these events and the change in your physical reality is something you are innately attracted to or the events and change are related to something you dread and fear, in both cases you should know that the energy you provide in the form of reaction feeds the "spell" being cast. This energy strengthens the vibrational pull and more readily creates the particular physical reality being broadcast to you.

While your world is not replete with devils, as many of your religions would have you believe, it is in fact full of what we shall call "wizards" who are continually attempting to cast spells through the use of vibration and frequency in order to create a world environment that they themselves can manipulate and control. We will not get into a discussion here with regard to who these wizards actually are but suffice to say that they are not who you think they are and they are not necessarily good, bad, right or wrong. Certainly however, they are being directed and unconsciously manipulated by influences that have specific intention related to the lowering of consciousness, slowing of the process of Ascension and the ushering in of a lower density, new Third Dimensional timeline.

It is important therefore, to understand how reality is created in order to control your own personal destiny, the destiny of your friends and families and the destiny of the planet as a whole, particularly as the current timeline transforms and as Ascension energies become more intense. If you are fearful of what you are hearing and the words that are being spoken all around you, realize that this is an attempt to manipulate you – to cast a Spell on you in order that the creation of what you fear be further generated in your physical environment. On the other hand, if you are in favor of what you hear, it is quite possible that you are also being manipulated in order to increase the energetic intensity and propel these events into physical reality for your own Soul purposes.

Whatever your perspective or Soul desire, first and foremost become conscious of the nature of vibrational frequency in the attraction and creation of your personal reality, the reality of your community and the physical reality of your world. Pay close attention to the sounds of words and phrases that you speak and that you hear. Notice when what you are hearing triggers negative feelings and fearful emotions; Monitor your own words for their vibrational content and stand up to what you hear around you through an understanding that you are the one in charge of your vibrational and emotional output. Do not fear, do not adhere and do not lend your energy by virtue of your attention to any thought or anyone that does not resonate for you at a Soul level. Learn to be mindful.

Next, it is important to tune out the particular vibrational frequencies you distrust. In this case stop speaking or listening to words and messages you deem unqualified. Rebuke the "Spell" being incessantly cast upon you through repetition in any form or via any vehicle of technology. Learn to be conscious of efforts to elicit your emotional response.

It is time to close down the frequency-instigating channels and banish the vibrational manipulation, particularly if you find the words and vibrations untruthful and especially if they somehow generate fear in you or in others. By dampening the message and the sound, the vibrational frequency is lessened and its power is curtailed. In this way you are no longer contributing to a negative mass conscious vibration, nor are you allowing the message to gain personal access to you through the natural laws of reality attraction.

Become conscious of the power of words and sound to generate vibrational frequencies that can manipulate, from wherever or whatever place they may originate. Understand the potency of sound, words and phrases, and recognize their relationship to your personal vibration and frequency. Take control and master your own vibrational output. In doing so, retrieve the power stolen from you so that you can hinder and even halt the potentially detrimental manipulative vibrations being used to cast a "spell" upon your world reality.

Group Intention and Reality Manifestation

Each individual attending or cooperating in a gathering or a group is present not only by conscious choice, but for purposes related to his or her own Essence Path, mission and unconscious goals. However, once a group forms, it generates its own mission, goal and energetic resonance, and in many cases focused conscious intention arising from the hearts of several or many individuals joined in a group can have a far reaching impact on reality.

For the most part therefore, group gatherings are never accidental, rarely inconsequential and their importance should not be overlooked. When individual thought and energy are unified, organized and focused in a group format, a new tangible power arises from the intentions generated. Because thought forms, goals and missions expressed by a group demonstrate an oscillation that increases exponentially with each individual, the potential for reality manifestation by a group is maximized. Thus the group's ability to manifest its goals, desires and intent in reality, whether by conscious desire or not, is greatly enhanced. We would go as far as to suggest that aside from physical survival of the young, this is perhaps the true basis of the family units you know, at least from a metaphysical perspective.

Naturally, as we have often reminded you this effect can originate from either a positive or negative polarity, and it should be remembered that fear and challenges expressed by a group are just as readily manifest in reality (if not more so) as faith, desire and goals that have a positive benefit. This is the reason that group motivation and desire is an important consideration, as the emotional and energetic content found therein is quickly propelled into your world.

It is not by happenstance that many of your religious and esoteric practices not only call for individual prayer and meditation they base much of their philosophy on the power emanating from group prayer, organized gatherings, unified thought and directed meditation. A well-known biblical adage confirms that when two or more people come together in unified thought or prayer, their request is more readily addressed by "God." This is because a vortex of energetic desire is created by group action that maximizes the potential for reality creation and manifestation (known or unknown to the subjects).

It is immaterial whether you believe the manifestation that occurs, whatever form it takes, is a gift from the God source or merely a physical representation of your own conscious intention. In either case the fact remains that group prayer, meditation and focused thought increases energetic and vibrational potential, and this maximizes a thought form's power to magnetize and sculpt the creative particles necessary to generate reality's miraculous unfolding.

In fact, we would say that although group gatherings large and small take place worldwide constantly (in conscious forms you understand and unconscious forms you may not) and are commonplace, it is unfortunate that the truth about methodology and the power of such gatherings to create reality are not better understood and more willingly utilized. We would suggest that this is perhaps not unintentional. Indeed, many political, religious, governmental and other authorities that understand the true magnitude and power of group energetics, particularly those wishing to directly control the reality manifestations of internal groups, work actively to stifle such understanding. To do so, much of the esoteric literature, and many of the meditative practices and philosophies you are taught, are at the very least misleading seeking to divert you from accurate and truly valuable forms of prayer, group or otherwise.

As an example, from the youngest age most are taught to beseech an invisible force to answer their personal needs and desires. Usually, such emotional requests are for those things that are not present in life and the request originates from the fear of what you either do not have or do not want in your life. Because fear is so emotionally charged, such prayer is also emotionally charged, and such a prayer request is akin to sending an energetic message to the Universe asking it to reinforce the very things you are fearful, you will not or do not have. Generally, the result is a continuation of the fear, or "lack", which is embedded in your state of fear.

Remember that the Universe does not judge and therefore does not see a specific condition or state as good, bad, right or wrong. It knows only that you, as a co-creator of your reality, are sending out emotionally charged thought forms, which you wish to be attracted into your reality. Like attracts like. For this reason, we would advise you to refrain from prayer and meditation that is fear-based, or that demands a redress of your current reality. Such prayer and focused thought, whether by an individual or by a group, works to reinforce the state of lack you wish to leave (please see the discussion on editing down from wholeness entitled "Becoming Whole" in Chapter 6).

Instead, although it may seem counterintuitive, we would suggest prayer or meditation that offers a grateful acknowledgement of your situation and a conscious understanding of your state's relevance to your higher growth. Then in conjunction with this, focus an expression of your truest firm belief (and faith in the Universe, or God if you prefer) that not only will you achieve what you desire, but it is also already present and available to you in all ways, even if it is not visible. Such a method of prayer and focused intention is far more productive to changing your current state.

Misdirection of focused thought and prayer deadens the real potential that exists to achieve a rewarding life experience, which is the ultimate gift possible as each individual masters their ability to co-create reality. This is magnified greatly within the potential inherent in prayer and meditation performed jointly or by a group.

Why is this so? Because groups at all levels that come together in unified prayer and meditation, especially those that understand the power behind their energetic projection, increase the magnetism of their desires by creating an energetic vortex of sorts. Once created, that vortex has an augmented ability to attract any desired goals (prayers) into reality. In addition to this, when speaking of Ascension mechanics, such group focus augments aspects of energetic communication between you, the planet's electromagnetic grid and your Soul matrices. This allows an increase in higher levels of guidance available to you.

This also works inversely to increase the grid's power and, in its wake, pushes the energy grids of the planet to higher vibrational resonance. At the current time this is highly productive if not critical to the planet and the Solar System's dimensional transcendence, as it facilitates the evolutionary process that raises all Universal Dimensions an octave and, ultimately, will serve to propel the dimension into Ascension evolution.

Let us add one other important and perhaps unknown aspect to our conversation concerning the power of group intention. Although it is true that human existence in the Third Dimensional realm for the most part allows each entity to participate in the process of their own Soul's evolution and growth as co-creators of their reality and environment, it is true precisely because human and planetary energetic structures are aligned thus allow this to be so. These structures, which are both physical and energetic in nature, are highly organized and unified, linking each individual, each group and all beings to the planet and subsequently to the farthest reaches of the Universe.

First of all, be aware that Earth, your Solar System and your Galactic sector are designated as the home of Human Angelic Souls. The DNA of Human Angelic's is therefore coded to be in perfect synchronicity with the electromagnetic grid of the planet Earth. As part of this alignment, the energetic human Chakra structure, which is each individual's personal energetic grid and higher communication system, parallels and is linked with the structure of the energetic Chakra system and electromagnetic grid of planet Earth.

It is human DNA that acts as a scalar communications link between an individual's Chakra system and all the cells in an individual's body. In turn, the Chakra system of the individual is further organized to communicate and link with the Earth's Chakra system and electromagnetic grid. This communicates an individual's vibrational resonance (formed by thoughts, emotions, fears, desires, as well as higher purpose and goals, etc.) to the Universe, and it is this link that magnetizes the particles that pull your reality into creation.

The manifestation of reality is therefore based on the vibrational communication it has received by virtue of this system. Finally, there is a two-way street of communication between each person's Chakra System, Earth's Chakra System and electromagnetic grid and the Universe at large, which includes one's Soul or Higher Self and, ultimately, the God Source itself.

Because of this, all Human Angelic incarnates in your world (unbeknownst to them) act as channels of sort, communicating what is desired to the Earth grid and the Universe, while receiving guidance and information from the Universe via Earth's Chakras and the subsequent personal "download" you receive via your own Chakra system. There are overlapping considerations to be sure, but this is the main reason it is so important that these energetic systems, including your individual Chakra system as well as the electromagnetic grid of planet Earth, be open and unencumbered by interference.

In this regard, the environment in which you exist today is problematic at best, as it grossly interferes and tampers with these natural avenues of energetic communication, diminishing your access to higher guidance as well as dampening the internal communication of your own Chakra system, your DNA and your cellular structure. It is important to be aware of this and to work towards combatting the environmental effects through the care and maintenance of your physical and energetic body, as well as by care and consideration for the Planet's well being whenever and wherever possible.

We have provided you here with some understanding of just how group gatherings, focus and intention can augment the channels of energetic communication, increasing power and potential so that what is desired may be beneficially propelled into reality in your world. By knowing that the focused energy originating from group intention has the power to activate the Earth's Chakras and grid system in extraordinary ways, facilitating reality's manifestation, you are well on your way to understanding your true power and the importance of your choice in participating at a group level. Add to this the ability of a group to increase planetary vibrational resonance (through the Earth Chakra and grid structure) as well as the timeliness of such energetics when seen through the evolutionary process known as Ascension, and you have the basis for understanding why joining together in focused desire, thought, intention, prayer or meditation is so powerful.

Chapter 6
Earthly Existence - On Health, Relationships and Moneyy

Becoming Whole

You are miraculous beings. The life force that is "You" is derived from the energy of your Soul. That energy is transferred to the physical body via the etheric or energetic body, which communicates to your vital organs, via your chakra portals, with the assistance of your DNA, which further communicates the energetic instructions it receives to all aspects of your cellular structure.

We have told you in the past that DNA acts as a two-way antenna and the etheric body, meaning the energy body, does in fact communicate with your physical being through your DNA, just as your DNA communicates back to your energy body its state and condition. Thus, for the most part, your DNA loyally communicates to the cells in your body the instructions it has received from your energetic or etheric body and generally this is the condition that is ultimately revealed and pressed into human physical form.

It is for this reason that we have said many times that almost all chronic dis-ease or physical dis-comfort (removing for a moment a discussion of traumatic injuries) can be said to originate from a lack of communication between the energetic or etheric body and the physical being. In fact, it is energetic blockage within the communication process that ultimately leads to physical body discomfort. How is this possible? Let us explain.

First of all, in physical reality, you should be aware that all that is possible exist already. In other words, all that is possible is present in the physical, within your grasp, within your ability to perceive it and within the reality itself. Thus, the energy coming from your Soul through your energetic body is perfect in nature.

However, when this energy transfers to the physical being, blockage in the chakras causes your physical being to "edit-down" from all that is possible and all that exist. This means, once in physical awareness, you edit down from wholeness and from perfection. The resulting block located within a chakra, body part or area is a type of "guardian" that you have placed in order to "edit-down" the all-ness that is being transferred to you.

Why would you do so? Generally it is for reasons related to your mission in the lifetime, your goals for growth or your karmic endeavors. That is to say if there is a reason for you to experience certain issues and "lacks", whether they be health, financial, emotional or the like, the perspective of lack serves as an opportunity for growth. Based on pre-chosen events, the environment you grew up in and your learned responses, among other things, you have edited-down from all-ness so that you may be provided with a certain perspective and the parameters for an issue to be made present in your life. By editing the energy down, you have created a personal vehicle for growth in whatever area of your life you have edited down.

But this need not be your final lot in life. Naturally, if you have chosen this, which in most cases you have prior to the lifetime for significant karmic growth lessons, then, it is possible that this is something you must experience as ordained by you and your Soul, God if you prefer that terminology. But this is rare to be sure, especially now in this age of Ascended energies.

In many cases, the process of editing down is spontaneous due to newly formed belief structures that have been superimposed on you, electromagnetic and environmental factors or other blockages that have taken from in the energetic exchange between the etheric body and the physical body. These blocks can be removed through free will, by the grace of God, and you have the ability to edit-up rather than edit-down if only you do so via your conscious intention.

Thus, as an example, if all wellness and all health that can be had exists already, and your dis-ease is caused by energetic blockages in the information coming to the physical structure that creates an edited down health presence, you can just as easily edit up to all wellness and health. Naturally, this requires conscious intention and energetic as well as real physical effort, since once a blockage of this nature has manifested within the physical existence, in essence it is a reality with which now must be dealt.

As we said, it is not possible for us to discuss here the myriad of reasons an individual might edit down from all-health. Sometimes this is related to growth and sometimes it is related simply to a misalignment of the energetic body. Often times it is because the higher self has deemed that the life purpose is accomplished and thus physical existence is no longer necessary. In such a case, the Soul begins to recede and slowly pull its energy out of the physical being through the etheric body. We understand that this is not a subject most are comfortable with due to your current focus in physical reality and your perspective that makes the physical body the sum total of who you are in the Universe, though please understand that this is not accurate or true.

What is important is the understanding that you have the ability through your belief and your conscious intention (Will) to reinvigorate and recharge the communication between your DNA and your cellular structure, your DNA and your etheric body and the etheric body and your Soul. How is this accomplished? Let us suggest that this is first and foremost a matter being within one's Essence and on one's Essence Path. Being in one's Essence is related to being in the now with the conscious understanding that one is doing the work of one's Soul, rather than the work of one's Ego.

More importantly, since many have questions with respect to how one actually heals, the manner in which healing is effectuated, as we said the most important aspect of this is the belief in editing-up to wellness and healing as opposed to the continual editing down of your health status. There are many ways to effectuate this, but all of them have a common denominator: belief that all wellness and all healing is already present in physical reality and has been accomplished.

In your Essence, in the "Now", believe with all your heart and emotional content that wellness is achieved and prosperity is present. Regardless of what your logic and rational thinking tell you, communicate this message back through your cellular system via your DNA, through the chakras that may be blocked, and tap directly into the energies of your etheric body and your Soul. Pull the all-ness of your Soul's energy through the body, and bring them forth into the physical structure, changing the vibrational patterns, eliminating the energy blockages and revealing wholeness to any situation.

Miracles are accomplished everyday both by individuals and by groups. Group energies in this respect are invaluable for as a Master once said: "If two or more of you agree on anything and ask, then it will be given." Coming together in groups to envision wholeness, to envision healing and to believe that it is actually present with you in the Now is paramount to achieving wellbeing and wholeness. Have you not wondered why when you are in a group situation, where everyone is feeling a certain way, you pick up that feeling? Why you are able to leave the group and continue on for however long with that feeling and that energy? It is because the feeling (energy) that has been transmitted to you is a powerful healing that you have taken on and resonated with. In essence, you have edited up (or down as the case might be) to that energetic level.

What is a difficult and unfortunate thing is that though many will see something or feel something or think something together with others in the Now, hours later they are swayed back to thinking or feeling or seeing something in a manner that forces them to lose the center and grounding they had previously achieved. In fact, they have re-found their original "editing." The objective then in true healing is to change one's editing perspective, maintain one's center position and open up to the wholeness that is available – editing UP to all wellness, all abundance, all health, all happiness and all love. And more importantly, remember to consciously maintain that energy, that belief, that feeling and that faith as you move forward without being swayed or knocked off your feet as you walk through the proverbial village.

If you can do this and learn this conscious process of being then you have not only learned how to center, ground and retain a conscious emotional connection to yourself, you have learned how to tap into your energetic body, dispelling blockages that may occur between the energetic body, the DNA and the body's cellular structure. The quality of your vibration improves as you consciously connect to your Soul. And when you have reached a certain vibrational quality, dis-ease, negativity and evil can no longer sense your presence because blockage in the communication emanating from your energetic body to your physical structure is no longer possible.

You are miraculous Creators in that through your feelings and your thoughts, through your emotional content and your belief structure, you have the ability to change the fabric of your reality and the makeup of your world. This begins with a change in your own physical being whether it be the healing of illness or the changing of your state and status in the world. Believe that health is already present within you. Believe that wellness is already present in your body. Believe that abundance and prosperity are already in your hands. Believe that love, tenderness and joy stand in front of you right now. This is the process of creation and wholeness is the condition most akin to the natural state that connects you not only to your world but also to your energetic body and your higher self. This is the key to a life that is satisfying and fulfilled, a life filled with the "all-ness" of all that is possible in your world.

The Question of Relationship

Many times the question of "relationship," one you have with another individual or one you have with a group, comes into play. We would like to explore with you the basis for many of those relationships.

First of all, it should be understood that each entity entering into physical incarnation comes with a particular set of desires and goals that it wishes to accomplish in the lifetime. These desires and goals are generated in various ways, but one of the principal vehicles used for achieving life goals are the "extenuating circumstances," shall we call them, created via the various relationships you form. These extenuating circumstances are most often generated when in conjunction with your Soul you form experiences of mutual participation with other Souls who participate with you along the way. These relationships, or sometimes their absence or lack, formulate the basis of what become substantial opportunities for growth in the lifetime of a particular individual.

As such, during the lifetime, each Soul, individually and with individual intent, has what we have termed in the past "Soul Mates" (for the purposes of this discussion, let us overlook for now other important levels of Soul participation, which include Souls that originate from the same Soul group or matrix, as is generally the case among other things). Soul Mates, who might also be described sometimes as Task Mates, are those Souls that have through Soul contract or for the purpose of energetic (karmic) balancing decided to participate with you at some point during the lifetime in a way specific to growth for either you or the other Soul. Generally, and not to discount free will, which allows you to bypass or negate such contracts during the actual unfolding of the lifetime, these are the individuals and in some cases groups with whom you have life relationships in one way or another.

It is unfortunate that Soul Mate in your vernacular has come to mean a love object or a person you desire, or even a person who is closely related to you or associated with you in terms of liking what you like and being your friend. While this can be true, usually nothing could be further from the truth. You should be aware that the basis of a Soul Mate relationship from the perspective of your Soul is NOT the individual who likes the same things you like or wants to do the same things you want to do. On the contrary, more often than not, your Soul Mate is that relationship that provides you with the maximum opportunities for growth, and as such can sometimes push your predispositions in extraordinary ways.

In many cases, in fact in the majority, that growth and the relationship are charged with important dynamics that originate through the volatile situations and difficult challenges coming out of the relationship. Again, although this is not always the case and it must be remembered that a Soul Mate is most likely an entity known to you at a Soul level who supports your growth unconditionally, generally Soul Mates are those individuals in the lifetime who provide you with extraordinary challenges. In important ways they participate with you, unconsciously, in difficult and often extreme situations intended to provide you with either the development of certain aspects of your character or for long-term growth within the lifetime.

We have discussed in the past how an entity creates the basis of their Life Path prior to the lifetime. In conjunction with this, you understand that aspects of your personality are developed in childhood and are formed as a result of your childhood environment, including your parents (many of whom, for better or worse, are indeed Soul Mates), your siblings and the environmental parameters that forge your personality features. You know also that these features play an important role in your perspective and how you see the world, which also plays prominently in the events you create and the polarity (positive or negative) from which your Essence Path and life mission unfolds.

What may be unclear to you, however, is just how a Soul Mate contributes to the creation and unfolding of your Essence Path and your life mission. As an example, take a domineering parent who was always critical of you, refusing any demonstrations of love or affection, and always demanding more. Now imagine that one of your purposes in the lifetime was to work on issues of self worth and pride. Clearly, that parent has accomplished their work well, albeit in a seemingly challenging way for the child, and then the adult that is you.

Few among you would admit that such a parent was a "Soul Mate" but the fact remains that the parent acted in accord with your prelife agreement in order to instill in you the personality features necessary for your to work on the issues of self worth and pride. Similarly, those who find themselves abandoned by their parents, either through death or through actual abandonment, might provide any entity looking to a life lesson based on learning the lessons of acceptance and rejection with an invaluable head start in learning the principles of such an issue.

In this way, and despite the fact that in many cases this is accomplished through sometimes difficult, even tragic events and situations, Soul Mates nevertheless are those who have a special relationship with you that has nothing to do with similarities or things you all agree upon. It is in cooperation with "Soul Mates" that your particular polarity, your life mission and your personality traits are developed and explored. In this manner, you come together in relationships whatever their nature or outcome in order to provide each other with specific opportunities for growth related to your Soul purpose.

We would further this discussion by stating that in many cases when the desired opportunities have been fulfilled, often relationships have then served their original intention. In such a case, they become neutralized and many times there will no longer be a magnetic charge holding each individual to the other. In these cases, relationships wane and individuals grow apart or move on. Sometimes however, relationships that have reached their purpose are neutralized in such a way that they seem to take on new life and it seems as though the relationship is revitalized and different. When this is the case, usually these relationships remain in tact and are important to the individual life long. It is also in these instances that the true Soul Mate experience is enjoyed, where through a neutralization of the originating bond, individual relationships transcend and are at last understood as from your Soul's perspective.

This also occurs in difficult relationships when an individual understands, through unconditional love, that what a parent or particular person did was most likely by arrangement. Challenging though the relationship was or is, the individual is now free of that bondage and able to reach a state of understanding. This is one of the reasons forgiveness is of such value to you, since understanding that there are reasons that conscious reason may not know allows one to forgive the individual and the situation (acknowledging that this is most probably a Soul Mate who treated you in this or that manner at your behest). Such awareness creates a state of grace that allows the individual to transcend the situation and, in many cases this neutralizes all connection to the other. Often it also eliminates the need for you to continually repeat that particular pattern of growth through a never-ending chain of similar relationships.

But why else have we chosen to bring this discussion of relationship to the forefront currently? It is for this reason. In the energetic (Ascension) environment in which you find yourselves today, the participation and opportunities each entity may have with another is sped up and maximized. In many cases, the relationships you have, and sometimes the fallout from them, are intensifying in ways that you have not experienced prior to now.

Most importantly, we would like to explain that just as you have Soul Mates in the individual sense, so too relationships of this nature can form between groups or between a group and an individual. Opportunities of this nature can be identified by situations where one group of individuals provides and participates in opportunities that might give the individuals in another group opportunities for growth.

While we cannot say that when this occurs at a group level there is always a basis of Soul recognition as with a true individual Soul Mate, it is important to know that groups when they organize and form also have an Essence Path and life mission, as well as some sense of what the individuals contained within it are seeking for growth. While this might not be wholly individual in nature, it does pertain to the group since as we have said before, groups, families, communities, races, cultures and countries all have group missions and purposes in much the same way an individual does.

All of these groups then are intermingling constantly and participating with each other at various levels in order to provide themselves and the individuals that comprise it growth as part of an overall purpose. Sometimes, this happens in ways that are harmonious, but at other times, as is the case with individual Soul Mates, these group "relationships" can be extremely challenging and difficult. While this applies to companies and organizations, it can also apply to cultures, religions, countries and continents. One need look no further than the extreme political situations found in your day to day politics, in the severe extreme positions of different religious groups worldwide, or the seemingly uncooperative nature of cultures, races and whole nations to verify the validity of this. In such a way, one might say that the conflict that ensues between these groups, as well as within it, is far from casual or accidental in nature.

In times such as these, where evolution through Ascension is apparent throughout your Galaxy and in a time where energy is augmented and must as a matter of physics be discharged and dispelled, there have been and will emerge vast "opportunities" for group interaction and participation throughout the world. Some will be inconsequential, some will be harmonious and some will be extremely challenging.

When these interactions occur, bring to mind our discussion of "Soul Mates." Acknowledge and understand at those times that much like Soul Mates, when various diverse groups interact and global situations arise the opportunities for growth, both from an individual and a group perspective are abundant. More difficult still, remember that many of these world growth occurrences have universal purpose in providing all participants on every side with opportunities for growth, despite the fact that the events generated may seem to shake the very core of Third Dimensional Earth.

The Money Paradigm

Let us begin by stating an old spiritual adage – one you have undoubtedly heard used in some form or another - "The love of money is the root of all evil." This saying was not arrived at by happenstance, and it could also be said that this phrase is a verbal demonstration that when it comes to the principles of "money" and monetary success many of you have empowered an object of little real significance with a relevance that is out of control in your world today.

First and foremost, be assured that the issue of which you speak is one pondered and shared by many of you. The concept of money, and the experience of energetic exchange that it once represented, has outlasted its worth and is no longer compatible with the higher consciousness that is now dawning.

Thus, its existence is drawn into question. As you enter a new Golden Age, those elements of your culture and society that are no longer relevant, valid or based in truth, such as the concept of money and success, begin to collapse. Thus you will begin to see in the broader reality around you drama and turmoil, particularly that related to the concept of money and the world of finances related to it. In fact, were you to see it from our perspective, you would see that the systems you have created regarding worth, success and gain are, in fact, in the process of collapsing. Though it is kept alive in the short-term by those who have a great stake in the continued viability and success of the system, within approximately a 25 year-period it will disintegrate as a viable measure of your worth or your world, and ultimately money will have no truth, validity or basis in your emerging reality whatsoever.

What you are experiencing when you have difficulty attracting money is your own Higher Self weaning you from a misguided attachment, as well as the fear of financial instability it generates, while pushing you towards Faith and the emergence of a new system of value and worth. In the process, and in the absence of the old monetary standards and paradigms that will shortly be no longer valid or relevant in your lives (due to their absence), you are given an understanding through life experiences that not only will you survive and continue to be taken care of, you will thrive, even amidst a lack of that which you fear you do not have enough of, money.

As this transition takes place, there is in your world a disillusionment based on finances (what it offers, what it procures and what it can no longer achieve or attain) and the collapse of standards that are no longer valid are being substituted by your own ability to survive without them or have what you need in your life created as you need it. This is in contrast to your previous need to have a warehouse of "money" to lull yourself into thinking that you had the possibility of procuring your every need when the time came. Instead, you are learning to manifest what you actually need as you need it, rather than horde a fictitious item that is relatively benign but that you have empowered.

You are being shown the truth of what it is to have Faith versus what it is to be constantly in a state of Fear; Faith that you will not be able to manifest in your life what you need without hoarding a disembodied paradigm, rather than your belief that you will be able to manifest easily and quickly whatever you do not yet have available in your life. In the process, you are forced to learn the principles of reality manifestation as well as the creation of your needs through Faith and not through Fear.

Thus you wrangle with yourself, for though you are approaching the time when you will readily have the ability to manifest daily what is necessary for your life to be happy and satisfied, your former attachment to the concept of money and the long gap needed to make it "real" makes you fearful that you will not have what is required from day to day. Though necessary in a lower Third Dimensional resonance reality, the concept of preparing for a rainy day has become pervasive in your beliefs. But in the emerging Ascended vibration of higher dimensions that you are entering such precaution is no longer relevant. Yet this remains problematic for you, since disengagement from the existing paradigms, which continue to hold relevance for many, has not been achieved. This will continue to be so until you discover a new way of thinking about your own survival and until such time as everyone is on the same page, meaning the time when collapse of the old, outmoded and prior untrue model is widespread and complete.

We assure you that if you have a belief that money and finances will ensure your survival, you are probably in for a great surprise as those systems that you believe in move closer and closer towards collapse. Therefore, in a manner of speaking, you are being guided to expand your consciousness and have Faith that whatever form your finances take you are assured the essentials and things needed for your happiness and survival. While we admit this seems a challenging place to be right now, particularly in a culture and society that has come to worship money's existence, you are being led to discover that survival and even wellbeing are not necessarily financially based but rather come to you as a matter of your own Faith and feelings of stability, security and prosperity.

To answer your second question, we would suggest that you practice seeing yourself secure and stable, as we have said, for now more than ever before thought is action in motion. That which you think is that which your cells resonate, and that is what you will attract and manifest in your life. This is not an invitation to endlessly think about the idea of "money" and expect that you will attract money, as many have been led to believe. It is however an invitation to think of yourself as happy, see yourself provided for, experience the sensation of feeling stable and secure and focus your thoughts, as actions, into reality expression in your world. If you do so, whatever form is necessary for you to be happy, stable and secure will find you whether it be based in the paradigms you have empowered, that of money and gold, or seashells and beads for that matter.

Therefore, we suggest that in this instance you take your attention off of any particular object you wish to attract, particularly objects such as money where too many have already placed their power erroneously, and bring your power of creation back to yourself and your wellbeing. This will assist you to reprogram your beliefs and in its wake restructure your cellular resonance. Believe, with all your heart, that you will be well, you will be happy, you will be secure, you will be loved and you will be fulfilled. This is the true meaning of having "Faith," and in doing so you attract the things that are necessary to keep you happy, secure and fulfilled. If one of those things happens to be a certain financial state or status, then so be it.

But we caution you that those who have put their power and belief into objects such as money, things that only have power because all of you agree they do in the current moment, will be very disappointed as consciousness awakens and the world discovers there is no truth or validity to be found in these objects or precepts. Wean yourself from the attachment and focus on monetary amounts, vast monetary sums or various specific possessions, and learn instead to manifest the feelings, sensations, truths, events and actual realities that bring you satisfaction and happiness. In this way you will create what you need in your life, things that currently you rely on money to procure. Moreover, this will help you to be spared the let down of a system that is no longer based in truth and leaning towards collapse. To paraphrase another old adage, money, as well as many of the cultural standards and paradigms you have come to count on, such as your world financial system, does not bring you happiness, and such attachments may prove fleeting and inconsequential in the coming age.

 **CHAPTER 7**

FEAR, FAITH AND PHYSICAL REALITY CREATION

Finding Your Way to Neutral

You are miraculous beings living in miraculous times. But often, such times, and the people, events and discussions they spawn, can be seen as difficult, challenging and evocative. So how do you find your way to Neutral, in a world seemingly beyond your control?

When events are seen through the eyes of Faith (of the universal kind and not the religious type) with the understanding that perhaps there is a greater plan and a higher purpose at work, is it really appropriate to call such things "bad," "difficult" or "wrong." Or are the events and situations that transpire, challenging and misguided though they may seem, a product of what you and the many Souls around you are creating in order to explore certain quantum fields within the framework of mass consciousness. Is it possible that these things are created as a way to propel vast and diverse experiences into reality – experiences that must be met by you and at some point could serve as unique and individual opportunities for Soul growth?

Whatever you believe, far too often challenging events and times influence and sway you deeply, reaching down into the core of your daily belief systems and existence. Many of you find yourselves distracted and appalled by what happens around you. Others feel that the quality of their experience is suffering or that certain events, groups and individuals are beyond the pale. Too often many are brought to a state of Fear, afraid for their well-being or for the future of those they love, while others are disgusted and angered by events that seem infantile, arbitrary, uncontrollable and, often, unconscionable.

What is truly happening when these things are present in your life, as we have said in the past, is that reality, by way of the mass consciousness environment, is providing you with new opportunities that demand you to respond. Your Emotional Response becomes critical not only in how you navigate such experiences, but how they become embedded in your own reality via the events you attract to yourself.

While we are limiting our discussion today to events that seem external to your life personally, know that this is also applicable to the people, situations and events you meet on a daily basis in your close personal reality. How you process and react to the situations and events you witness is not only key to understanding the events themselves, it is a precursor of how and to what extent that experience develops for you in your world and your life. And because of this, the manner in which you emotionally meet and respond to them becomes a valuable gauge in identifying your own current level of consciousness and your vibrational resonance. If you will, your Emotional Response (the feelings, sentiments and emotions evoked) is a key expression of the maturity and quality of your consciousness. Let us explain.

First of all, you know by now that what many find arbitrary and accidental is anything but that. Everything that is created is manifest in your reality via vibrational attraction and with purpose. While this greater purpose cannot always be ascertained at the moment, rest assured that even the most seemingly inconsequential events have at their basis some reason that they have been electromagnetically drawn into and generated in physical reality.

The problem is that this "reason" is often related to a growth lesson that may not on the surface have much to do with you personally. In that respect and again limiting our conversation to those events widely generated through mass consciousness, if not for modern communications and instantaneous media feeds, you personally would probably not even be aware of half the things occurring in your world. For that matter, things happening across town or even down the street would probably not be readily known to you. In that case, you would have no Emotional Response to them.

In addition, you would not experience the emotional roller coaster ride that you are often forced to endure today, constantly asked to respond and even rate your emotional experience (like or dislike, happy or frowning Emoji, thumbs up or down). Most importantly, you would not be swayed or pushed into a state of fear, which is a vibrational-deadener, if we may be so bold. Certainly, you would not become emotionally drained and constantly pushed off balance, susceptible to all manner of coercion, manipulation and emotional prodding much as you currently are from the barrage of news, information, advertising and drama now delivered to you 24/7.

So what is really happening? Let us begin by answering the first part of the question we have posed. What can be the greater good related to the constant barrage of information, particularly that which concerns difficult and challenging events?

The answer to this comes in two parts. As we have said in the past, your world is currently experiencing Ascension, where many younger Souls will continue incarnating in lifetimes within a newly formed Third Dimension, rife with all manner of Third Dimensional learning experiences and lessons. The challenges you see emerging daily, which appear to you unlike any from the past, are an indication of this, as is the entrenchment of individuals on all sides of an equation who appear to dig in their heals refusing to see any side of an issue but their own.

As we have explained, these young Souls see the world as "Me and other Me's" and they would prefer to force everyone to believe what they believe and be like them rather than be open to any experience of tolerance, acceptance and unconditional love (attributes of older Souls). For these young Souls growth is almost always based on group interaction and karmic energetic balancing, something that would be difficult to obtain in a world that has independence, acceptance and unconditional love as its basis.

Meanwhile, the current Third Dimension is evolving and in time will transfer its energetic components to a higher vibrational resonance incorporating Fourth and Fifth Dimensional ideals and qualities. This includes those older Souls currently incarnated in the Third Dimension who have graduated in terms of their vibrational quality and who will in the future incarnate in a Fifth Dimensional world, but currently remain incarnated in the Third Dimension. Despite their Third Dimensional incarnation, these Souls seek to gain growth through individual endeavors rather than relying on group karmic balancing with others. Thus they have a more "laissez faire," independent expression and style of learning. Their motto is generally, "You are you, and I am I, and each of us are free to be what we choose, causing harm to none."

As Ascension-based evolution takes place, there is an overlap of these dimensions, as well as those older and younger Souls incarnated within them. Thus, more and more there will be young Souls firmly positioned in Third Dimensional Reality, who will continue on therein but who will find themselves side-by-side older Souls, who are destined to evolve after completing the current lifetime.

The great span and disparity of consciousness and belief that you see happening between people and groups all around you is indicative of this evolutionary pattern. In time however, as these patterns and groups delineate, like-minded will find like-minded wherever they are, and you will witness great movement of people, without them knowing exactly why, as they strive to find the like-minded people and communities with which they resonate.

Simply put, more and more today you discover people attempting to find "community", identifying, communicating and even moving to places where other like-minded individuals reside. This is occurring on both sides of the equation. Ultimately, this will further separate those remaining in a Third Dimensional environment from those evolving to the Fifth Dimension in future lifetimes. This will occur even though these individuals must continue on and complete their current incarnations in the Third Dimension, living together in the same physical world while doing so (whether this can be done peacefully and productively is yet another question).

This is also despite the fact that these individuals, older Souls if you will, are already exhibiting and utilizing Fourth and Fifth Dimensional ideals and standards while still continuing lives in your world. And it is precisely because of this that your world seems more separate, disjointed and divergent than ever before. It is perhaps for this reason that there seems to be a clash of civilizations, a struggle emerging between the old world and the new one; old religious dogma and new belief structures; the East and the West; the Industrial World and the Third World; the Haves and the Have-Not's.

Returning to our original question, we have often stated that Fourth and Fifth Dimensional attributes and sensitivities make one highly intuitive, and such sensitivity means that one is constantly aware of situations and events, as well as the emotions they evoke in the world around them. In higher dimensions, these things are experienced naturally as an added physical "sense" and instead of manually tuning into the 24/7 news-stream on a fabricated device, you are inwardly and intuitively aware of exactly what is transpiring in your family, your community and your world just by thinking of them and without the need for any communication device, social media pages or news feeds.

But such sensitivity and intuitiveness carries with it the awesome responsibility of protecting, controlling and managing your own Emotional Response and Energy Field, and this is what relates to our current discussion and question. In such a world, the ability to find Faith, peace and emotional Neutrality (boundaries if you will) becomes a high ideal if not a matter of self- preservation.

Thus in a sense, the external technology that currently affords you the ability to have an instant connection with your world and demands an immediate Response from you, in all its myriad of emotional colors, is in effect a training ground for what is to come for all those evolving to higher vibrational resonance and higher dimensional incarnations. If you will, this is a way for you to experience these events, including the emotional response that they evoke, as a form of "practice" for a future time where this knowing will be common place and a natural part of your inner talents and abilities. Surely, if you did not have control of your Emotional Response under such circumstances, you would have the greatest difficulty functioning in such a future environment.

So this leads us to the second part of the question. If having such immediate knowledge of things, events and people via externalized technology has the higher purpose of providing a kind of future emotional response "training," why are you thrown into torrents of fear, loathing and anguish? The answer to this is that in having such ability, whether it is technology driven as in the Third Dimension, or a natural inner sense as in the Fifth Dimension, it is vital that you become conscious of your emotional state and output. Moreover it is especially important not to be swayed or pushed into a state of Fear by the events, challenges and people you are witnessing.

Your most valuable guide here is your Emotional Response and in that respect all of the things you witness currently become lessons -- guidance working to assist you in finding understanding, calm and "Neutrality" when your Emotional Response is provoked. You are, in a way, being given the opportunity to take a step back before hitting the like or dislike button or forwarding that Emoji. You are being asked to be thoughtful and to feel, yes, but not to panic, fear, lash out or react. You are being shown the importance of finding a Neutral emotional response, or some close proximity. This is so even when in extreme disagreement or witnessing challenge and falsehood that you know inwardly must in time be corrected.

Many will likely scoff at such a notion. They would have you believe that you must react quickly, take a stand and, where necessary, resist change, challenges, people and events that go against you or disturb your core belief system in some manner and would view a Neutral Emotional Response as denial or disinterest. Certain public figures have even made the speed of rebuttal and their consternation a hallmark of the day. Yet this is a clear indication of a younger Soul unable to achieve Neutrality.

The inability to achieve what we shall term "Thoughtful Neutrality" (closely related to the vibration of unconditional love) demonstrates lower consciousness and, as a direct result, a lowered vibrational output. A lowered vibrational output inevitably leads to attracting and generating a more challenging reality. When reality is generated far from the Neutral spectrum it magnetizes future events and situations that have a corresponding resonance since these events are usually derived from the negative polarity, which, by virtue of a lower vibrational quality, are more challenging in nature.

To be fair and in truth, sometimes a strong response is needed, and in some cases one is indeed being asked to take a stand and resist violations of universal Truth (again, these instances are usually opportunities for growth that are being generated by you for you, or for a higher purpose related to your own Soul growth or the Soul growth of others around you). Even so, considered resistance expressed from a place of Peace and Neutrality is always inherently more powerful. It is never a product of Fear or loathing and it is never defensive. Such resistance derives power from its Neutral polarity. It leads others to respect and rally around it, and never attempts to dominate, bully or cajole.

If you have any doubts concerning the difference in Response, let us use as an example the experience, albeit one caused by considerable world tragedy, fear and shock, when Western leaders rushed to strike at the heart of the challenges they faced when confronted with an unprovoked attack on the very brain center of your world in New York City at the beginning of the 2000's. The mass conscious Emotional Response that event generated, in conjunction with leaders who pushed hard to exploit the Fear and loathing of the populace without using a leadership based on "Thoughtful Neutrality," propelled your world in a direction that is a hallmark of the early 21st Century, if not the century as a whole.

We would suggest that while the outcome might not have been extremely different overall, and those events might still have required a stand for Truth and the innocent, the various contributing events the world has faced since then could have been quite different if individual and group Emotional Response had been tempered with Thoughtful Neutrality. Clearly, this was not what was intended by the Physical System Lord's incarnated entities that found themselves in positions of authority and influence at the time.

That said, noble resistance is always based on a commitment to a higher vibrational Truth and understanding. As a result, meeting it calmly and thoughtfully provides Soul growth for all who are involved. However, achieving it requires that one first find Neutrality, allowing the response, emotional and otherwise, to originate from there rather than from Fear. Responses that are Fear-based and emotionally charged on the other hand will ultimately propagate and increase the challenges derived from what is feared. Thought, when propelled into creation by your Emotional Response, inevitably attracts into reality events that are similar in vibration, and when the thoughts and Emotional fuel are Fear-based, the learning experience is far more challenging.

Because of this, we suggest that you see your Emotional Response, whether to situations with your friends and families or to events you see in your neighborhoods, communities and world, as a test of your ability to either approach or find Neutrality. See your response, for better or worse, as a measure of your vibrational resonance and quality of consciousness. The closer you are to finding "Neutral" (call it thoughtful calm if you prefer), and a Neutral Response, the closer you are to an enlightened consciousness and a more pleasing and beneficial outcome.

We would further suggest that this is the true intention behind the philosophy that calls for you to "turn the other cheek." In fact, such a philosophy is a call to Conscious Neutrality rather than a call not to maintain your Truth, place yourself in harm's way or go into denial. As an added benefit, finding that same breed of noble Neutrality makes you more equipped to enact a fortified resistance to what is being perpetrated. In such a manner, you metaphorically stare down the provocateur without allowing your own energy to lend the event or person additional power via the intense fear and loathing you feel; A power, we would add, that invites the continued manifestation and even augmentation of the very thing you are fearfully reacting to.

If you find yourself swayed dramatically by the people and events you see appearing in or dominating your world, it would behoove you to examine what in that person or event has swayed you in this or that direction and why your emotional content is so charged. Do you feel defensive or threatened? Are you fearful and do you recoil and wish to hide yourself away? Or, like the Good Witch of the South in the 'Wizard of Oz', are you able to laugh and brush off the scary threats of the Wicked Witch of the West, telling her in bemusement to "...be gone, before someone drops a house on you..."

What is significant in this is that your Emotional Response, whether it be to minor and insignificant things happening to you in your day to day life, or to world altering events happening in your community or your world, is a key to understanding your own consciousness and the growth of your Soul. Better said, the true measure of your consciousness corresponds to your Emotional Response and vice versa.

Your ability to reach a Neutral or even a Semi-Neutral response while still able to consider what has transpired carefully and thoughtfully is a key indicator of not only your resonance and consciousness, but the quality of the things you yourself are creating in your world -- for yourself as well as for others against the backdrop of mass consciousness. If you find that your Response is one of Neutrality, one of love, one of forgiveness, one of understanding, then this truly signifies that you have reached a state of grace where you are beginning to evolve, accept and incorporate Fifth Dimensional attributes.

You may wonder why this particular time period holds so much importance. As we have said already, it is the time of Ascension, an evolutionary process undergone by the Universe, the Universal Dimensions that represent its known structure and the Souls and beings that inhabit them. As we have also explained, during such times, as some evolve and some do not, you will see greater and greater separation in your world, represented by the mindset of individuals, groups, communities, countries, cultures, religions and races.

Against such a backdrop, there will be those that are more fearful wishing to hold onto more density, and there will be those seeking Truth and becoming more en-lightened than at any time in the past. But one thing that will be shared by all is the new energetic intensity of the events that you witness.

It is unfortunate that this period also requires a higher degree of turmoil, which is a factor of the polarity tension inherent in such divisional evolution, separation and duality. This is unavoidable in your world, which is based on Third Dimensional duality, something that will remain a constant despite the Third Dimension's evolution.

Still, as you continue to be faced with the lower vibrational resonances swirling around you, become the conscious Master of your Response. In a good many ways, begin to see that your Response has much to do with the manner in which turmoil finds you in the first place. This is so not only in terms of vibrational magnetic attraction and the degree to which it has an impact on your life, but also in terms of its higher purpose within the context of your own Soul growth and the growth of others.

Meditate on using your Emotional Response in conjunction with your thought forms for your highest good as well as the highest good of mass consciousness and humanity at large. See the measure of how well you control your Emotional Response, given various external stimulus, as a test if you like. Or see it simply as a necessary fact of life. But do see it and the events being manifest in your world today as part of a universal Truth that requires your attention and Mastery in order for you to move through events and situations successfully at the present time.

Regardless of how you envision it, know that your Emotional Response has much to do with your vibrational resonance, and as you know, your vibrational resonance has the greatest impact on what you attract to yourself by way of experience. Despite your life mission, your Essence Path and the many other considerations that influence the events that take place in your life, karmic and otherwise, your Emotional Response is one of the primary areas where your conscious endeavor and Free-Will can take control and put you in charge of outcome. Emotional Response, together with your belief structure, which is where your thought forms originate, remains the primal spark influencing how reality is constructed and attracted to you, by you, in the clearest possible sense.

Finally, discover a precept of ancient wisdom that points to achieving Neutrality of Mind in order to find enlightenment, peace and balance. This has often been misunderstood as being impartial, feeling nothing, achieving "nothingness" or having no response in order to find happiness. These interpretations are incorrect. What it truly implies is that once you are able to tame your Emotional Response and find Thoughtful Neutrality in whatever comes your way, you have reached a point where your vibrational quality rises above the fray, and this is what keeps you from the clutches of Fear, anxiety and misguided, knee-jerk reactions.

This in turn provides you with the ability to respond from a higher level of consciousness -- to feel without being overcome, think pure thoughts without being overwhelmed, receive higher guidance without being confused. More importantly, it has the power to make you impervious to the schizophrenic emanations of lower vibrational frequencies that are constantly vying to establish a foothold in your world.

When this is achieved, you no longer feel tossed helplessly upon a rough ocean, forced to respond anxiously to the daily ups and downs, highs and lows and billowing fears being manifested and explored by younger Souls all around you. At such a point, you will find that you have reached a place of contemplative Neutrality, where your resonant state remains constant, your vibrational output is improved and, because of that, the physical reality you create and magnetize to yourself becomes more stable. This is the place of peace and enlightenment sought by so many, where joy, happiness and abundance via the reality you are generating and attracting to yourself are the most probable future outcome.

Where there is Light, Darkness cannot exist

Q: *I have been re-reading Timeline Collapse...as Donald wins the election (much to my dismay). The probable future does not look good. Reading about the fall of ancient Rome is one thing, but to be right here right now is another! Do you have any guidance?*

Once a Buddhist Monk and his students needed to pass through a certain village that was consumed by chaos. Neighborhood rivals had taken to rioting, and villagers were in the streets hurling obscenities, sticks and stones at each other.

The Monk instructed his followers to walk down the main thoroughfare through the fighting crowd, holding their heads high and remembering to be without fear, judgment or loathing. He informed them that after they had passed through the crowd, he would follow in their footsteps and meet them at the other side of the village.

Shaken but trusting their teacher, the students began their treacherous walk through the violent crowd. For a moment the fighting broke off, and a slight path opened for them. But as the students passed deeper and deeper into the crowd, they forgot the Monk's instructions, lost Faith in his words and became fearful for their safety. They began to lament that they could be swallowed up in this terrible chaos, and the violence could be directed towards them at any moment.

The students wrung their hands and began to tell each other that they would be far better off to fight their way through such a crowd. As their fears augmented, suddenly and without provocation the crowd fell upon the students and even worse fighting began. Trapped in the midst of the violence, the Monk's followers were forced to defend themselves however they could, and they ran through the chaos being beaten and abused as they attempted to reach the other side of the village.

Having finally reached a hill on the other side of the village, the students watched and saw that their Master had begun to proceed down the same treacherous path they had just taken. Seeing this they wailed, "Our Master is walking directly into that villainous riot, and he will surely be injured or perhaps even killed."

Then they watched in amazement and saw the Monk walk slowly through the crowd untouched and completely unnoticed. To their even greater surprise, they saw that as the Monk passed, villagers began to shake hands, make peace with each other and wonder out loud why they had been fighting in the first place. Calm and quiet took reign over the entire village, and people returned to their homes and businesses as if nothing had ever happened.

As the Monk reached his students on the other side of the village, they were perplexed and asked, "Master, why did the villagers beat us savagely when we walked through the crowd, but when you walked through it, there was suddenly calm and peace, and everyone forgot what they were fighting about?"

The old Monk looked lovingly at his followers and answered, "Where there is fear, there is darkness. But where there is light, darkness cannot exist."

There are several points this allegory makes. First, it gives evidence that your vibrational quality is your protection. Secondly, it informs you that your vibrational quality is contagious exponentially. Thirdly, it explains that Fear deadens your vibration, and drags you into the midst of turmoil since like-vibration will attract like-vibration.

All of these lessons will become important as you witness the transformation of your Third Dimensional realm through the evolutionary process known as Ascension. As we have explained, more and more there will be a separation of those destined to remain within Third Dimensional incarnations and those destined to evolve to incarnations on a Fifth Dimensional Earth, known as Terra, once the current lifetime is complete.

In the meantime, those older Souls who are of a higher consciousness are destined to remain surrounded by more and more younger Souls, for whom basic karmic interaction is the standard and the norm. This will become more noticeable as well as intense over the coming years. As the divide augments, older Souls will be dismayed and disillusioned as they begin to feel they are a minority in a world that has seemingly lost its order and its reason. They will quite frankly be disheartened by events where the values previously held high by all individuals of higher consciousness fall silent by the roadside, trampled by lower vibrational energy fields and individuals who profess incomprehensible (to older Souls) values and standards.

As we have detailed for you, this period where older Souls and younger Souls must cohabit lasts for approximately the next 300 years, with the greatest changes taking place through the 21st Century. During that period, you will find that you are forced to make a choice with increasing frequency and impact concerning where you stand, as well as where and with whom you wish to be.

We have told you many times that like attracts like. Those of similar vibrational fields will ultimately find others of similar vibration and Soul age. Great migrations will take place, as older Souls who can no longer tolerate the low karmic energies of younger Souls change domicile and move to regions where more like-minded individuals are the majority.

In saying this, it must be remembered that it always takes two to tango. With respect to vibrational signatures, this means that often what appear to you to be two opposing sides is actually two sides of the same coin. In other words and as an example, religious fanatics, regardless of the trappings or whichever doctrine or other tailored attributes they may have, are almost always individuals of the same vibrational quality regardless of being on opposing sides. Often the same goes for a particular political loyalty or any other delineation. In most cases, the oppositions are merely younger Souls choosing sides in order to take part in opportunities for growth that may be generated by their conflict. One side is not necessarily better or worse.

But as our allegory demonstrates, true opposition is not opposition as much as it is banishing Fear, remaining constant and achieving neutrality and peace. In this regard and as a means of identifying each other, remember that younger Souls have as their motto, "Me and other Me's" whereas older Souls have as their basis the standard, "You are you and I am I, and each of us should be allowed to pursue who we are in peace with harm to none." Older Souls abhor the kind of base energetic karma that younger Souls find valuable to their growth. In addition, older Souls will never force their belief system on anyone, whereas younger Souls will at every turn attempt to force everyone to believe and act just as they do.

So how does this relate to current events and the Ascension process that is taking place? It demonstrates that: 1) Younger Souls are proliferating worldwide who will continue on in Third Dimensional incarnations, regardless of which side of the aisle or coin they profess to be on; 2) It shows that Older Souls are cycling off the planet at an enormous rate, and they will evolve to higher dimensional incarnations; and 3) It demonstrates that demographic adjustments will find some individuals being drawn to more enlightened places with the like-minded, while others will consider themselves to be in the perfect environment, remaining where they are because, essentially, they have found vibrational compatibility.

What this means for North America, as we have detailed extensively in our book, "Timeline Collapse & Universal Ascension: The Future of Third Dimensional Earth and Fifth Dimensional Terra," is that a split of thought, culture and, above all else, Soul age, in the US means that the most probable future trajectory you are on may no longer include the concept of a unified nation. Nor, perhaps, is such a concept preferable or even viable under emerging circumstances, a conclusion that will become more apparent as probable future events transpire.

Remembering that generally events in your world are opportunities for Soul growth, what is taking place correlates directly to an increase in the desires of younger Souls for growth and the Ascension evolution we have discussed. Such events are a catalyst pushing older Souls and those of higher consciousness to ultimately choose that their next incarnation take place at higher dimensional levels rather than in the emerging environment known as the Third Dimension, where you are focused now. In the meantime and as a practical matter, it creates a need to seek out and join with like-minded fellows, leaving behind outdated standards and the old separations based on family, heritage, lineage, affiliation, culture, tradition and similar variables.

For those wondering where older Souls will congregate in the US based on the probable futures emerging, we bring your attention to the specific regional unions that will in time develop and be successful within former US territories. Specifically, this includes the Pacific Coast Union, which will be comprised of the current states of California, Oregon, Washington and parts of Nevada, as well as the New England Union, which will include the current states of New York, Connecticut, Rhode Island, Massachusetts, New Hampshire, Vermont and Maine.

In addition, there will be smaller but powerful regional independent states like the Chicago State Union that will include parts of former Wisconsin, Illinois and Michigan, the Texas Union, which will include the former state of Texas and parts of New Mexico, Oklahoma and Arkansas, the Florida State Union and the Hawaiian Independent State. These regions will be fairly prosperous by the mid 21st Century and some will act as safe havens for those of higher consciousness and vibrational quality.

Unfortunately however, civil war, lawlessness and violence will be the norm in most of the remaining former US territories. In such areas, small city or regional states will develop similar to those found in the historical period known as the European Dark Ages, where trade, travel and communication were disrupted and curtailed by fear, violence and isolation. Advanced technological interface will be the only saving grace for these territories, since travel and all real time physical interaction will become virtually impossible due to the dangerous and violent environments.

Events such as the great Western Economic collapse, the West's final defeat in World War III, the disintegration of Continental Europe, the bankruptcy and disintegration of the US Federal government in Washington DC and the turmoil of the second US Civil War will be the backdrop of mass consciousness from approximately the years 2017 to 2050. Indeed, it will not be until the direct intervention of Russia and China, at the behest of the new US regional powers in conjunction with Canada and Mexico, that law and order will finally be restored to all continental non-aligned former US territories (those regions not part of the successful regional states we have mentioned). Such measures will herald the invasion and foreign occupation of those non-organized former US states, while also reestablishing peace in North America after 2040.

Though these probable futures may sound disheartening and insurmountable to you, as you encounter these events remember that you will be instinctively drawn to the area that offers you the best advantages based on your Soul's mission and your unconscious personal desires. Per the allegory of our Monk, let your vibration be your protection. Remember that life goes on, and let your intuition and heart draw you closer to like-minded fellows, organizations, communities and groups. Refrain from being reactive, and try always to be proactive. Be open, be inclusive and allow yourself to be drawn to places where you will find the most growth. By doing so, if your vibration is high and you have banished your fears, you will find safety, wellbeing and happiness with your loved ones. Remember that these events are not accidental, but are part of the evolutionary process of the Third Dimensional realm (for better or for worse). You will be where you are called to be and where you have desired to be from the start. Have Faith.

Finally, recall that you are Beings of Light. And as you remember who you are, know that, "Where there is Fear, there is darkness. But where there is Light, darkness cannot exist."

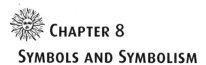 **Chapter 8**
Symbols and Symbolism

The Language of Symbols

You have numerous ways of communicating in your physical reality. Some speak one language. Others speak another. Some speak a few or many. But what you perhaps may not realize is that your psyche, what you term the conscious and the unconscious, also has its own language. That language uses Symbols and Symbolism as its primary components in much the same way letters and words form the basis of any spoken or written language. Naturally, the language of Symbols is an unspoken language but it has as much relevance and meaning as any verbal or written language you use.

The language of Symbols and Symbolism is the language that allows communication between the conscious you and the unconscious you, and, less realized, between the unconscious you and your Higher Self. When you are able to identify the meaning that is hidden in the Symbols and Symbolism that affect you, you are on your way to understanding the communications you are receiving, via your unconscious, from your Soul or Higher Self.

Symbols and their meaning can be generalized and agreed upon en masse in terms of outward appearance, but make no mistake they hold deeper meaning that is particular to each individual. This is because the language of Symbols is closely related to and based on your personal belief system, and particularly linked to the structure of your inner Core Values. It is through Symbols that your unconscious speaks to you, and through Symbols that your Higher Self is able to interpret what is taking place in your reality – a glimpse into your perspective, as seen through your conscious eyes. It is precisely for this reason that although Symbols are typically visual and sometimes mundane in nature, they are always proficient at generating an emotional state deep inside of you.

If you were to see Symbols as we do, you would see that even though they seem to be objects of benign focus in the physical reality, they are closely linked to the expression of your world. Since they are so closely attached to your feelings and emotions, they become a primary vehicle for communicating who you are. Symbols, or rather the feelings they trigger in you such as comfort, happiness, fear or rage, are often a truer representation of your personal "Truth" than any verbal confession or professed belief you might have concerning yourself.

Even if you have never seen them before and have no real idea what they mean, it should be understood that Symbols elicit emotional responses nonetheless. Often, this response is so deep as to not be known to you consciously. Regardless of that however, since emotion, whether it is conscious or unconscious, is vibrational in nature, it becomes closely linked to you at a cellular level. In other words, as you view a Symbol and your conscious or unconscious reacts and emotes based on the symbolism it contains, your cellular structure is vibrationally activated.

We have mentioned before that your cellular structure and your DNA serve as a kind of antennae constantly communicating with your Higher Self and sending as well as receiving messages to and from your Higher Self with regard to your state of being, your life mission, your physical reality, the mass consciousness environment and the success of your karmic endeavors. It is the emotional content and the vibration it causes in you that triggers this important messaging, and the Symbols you see everywhere almost constantly are endlessly providing stimulus to your emotional state at any given point in time. In some ways, your physical body is a walking vibrational communication device that is constantly updating your personal message and, via your unconscious, is always in touch with "home" base – your Soul.

Symbols then form the foundation of this messaging in as much as Symbols are responsible for the emotional content that is activating your cells and DNA. In this way, Symbols become the basis of not only who you are but also how you are expressing who you are in the world -- to others, to yourself and, perhaps of most importance, to your Higher Self. Have you never wondered why humans have such a fascination for the appearance of things? From one's own physical appearance, to the appearance of others, to the forms found in architecture and art, theater, film and entertainment, right down to what tattoo is placed where and how, how things appear has enormous importance. Although you may not recognize it consciously, the appearance of things is not actually important because of the look of the object. It is important because of the emotion these things – as Symbols -- elicit. That emotional content is a trigger that activates your cellular structure into a vibrational symphony communicating with yourself, your reality, your unconscious and your Higher Self.

Your Higher Self is always aware of your earth-bound state at any given point in time, and it interacts with you by sending you back acknowledgment of the emotional (symbolic) messages it is receiving from you. The messages sent back to you from your Higher Self come in the form of, as you may have guessed, Symbols. Such Symbols are delivered to you constantly in the dream state, in trance, during meditation, in prayer or even through synchronicity (a form of communication between you and your Higher Self that many of you now recognize as more than coincidence). In general, these Symbols, received in the myriad of ways we mention, can be seen as acknowledgment and communication directed to you and coming from your Higher Self via your unconscious.

In other words, these Symbols are a way of your Higher Self telling you that your message has been received. Additionally, it can be a way for your Higher Self to point out certain aspects not yet made conscious by you or, in some cases, may even represent guidance coming from your Soul. Ultimately, the exchange generates an unconscious vibrational attraction that literally magnetizes like vibrations to you manifesting events and situations in your life, becoming the true fabric of your reality. But that is another conversation completely.

Suffice to say that in communicating the Symbols that have meaning for you to your Higher Self, the unconscious does not focus on or emphasize the actual physical representation of the Symbol. This is why a Symbol can look one way to almost everyone, but have an infinite number of meanings depending upon the viewer and their personal interpretation. What is important is not the visual appearance of any given Symbol, but the sentiment, feeling or emotion attached to it and that it elicits in the viewer.

It is in this way, through the unconscious feelings and vibrational quality a viewer finds in any given Symbol, the Higher Self is able to perceive the experience of your reality. Many of you believe your guides and "angels" are watching over you, seeing what you are seeing in your every day life. This is never the case. Your guides, like your Higher Self, are not seeing with eyes but are "feeling" what you are feeling because your vibrational state, triggered by your emotions, is informing them of your current experiences.

In much the same way, because the feelings that a Symbol triggers in you have also been established by you personally, you are being guided when that same Symbol is returned to you and used by your Higher Self to communicate with you, expressed as it may be through the unconscious in a dream state, or in trance or meditation. Thus, a two-way communication has been created, and, more importantly, guidance from your Higher Self has made its way through to you — all with the use of Symbols. And this is precisely what we mean when we say there is a Language of Symbols and Symbolism.

While there are certainly many Symbols that are recognized en-masse and generally elicit similar emotions as agreed upon by mass consciousness, there is always a meaningful variation in the emotional content that is specific to each individual. However, even when a Symbol is well known and used widely, the individual aspect and meaning when they are used at the unconscious or subconscious level, delivered as they are from the Higher Self, can take on completely new and unique meaning and relevance.

Water, as an example, may have one general symbolic meaning for most individuals: Life giving, healthy, sustaining, thirst quenching, etc. Yet if you look closer, there are an infinite number of specialized meanings that can also be associated with the Symbol of water that may be relevant only to a particular individual.

Symbolism related to water could be pleasurable and life giving, or it could have an association for someone with fear, panic, disaster or even death. In this way, the emotional content contained in the Symbol for that particular person is what becomes communicated to the unconscious. The unconscious uses the association it receives to message the Higher Self and, in many ways, the Universe.

When the message is coming directly from the physical reality you are experiencing in the "Now", without having a past experience that is being transmitted to you by your Higher Self, it can also become the substance of a kind of vibrational "request" to your Soul and to the Universe. In this way, often the messaging of your experience to higher dimensional realms through your emotions can transform into intention -- a request that you make asking the Universe to send life events that assist you to experience "water" in this or that way.

As we have said many times, thoughts are actions. In this case, they can become intention propelled by emotional pleas to your Higher Self, as well as the Universe. The thoughts and emotional associations that Symbols evoke should be considered carefully since they may well have considerable impact on the events that emerge for you. It is for this reason that you should understand that your thought patterns should be monitored for content, emotional attachment and their possible creative (unconscious though this may be) impetus.

More often than not however, the emotion you are associating with a Symbol may actually be a component of your Soul's message to you. What originates that messaging is unique to each Soul and each person, but using our example of water associated with the emotion of fear, this would generally signify that in the lifetime or in a lifetime closely related to you water was responsible for your demise in some way. Perhaps a flood wiped out your town or your food supply causing you to starve, or you were drowned on the open sea, or quite the opposite, died of dehydration. What is important to see here is that the Symbol has become a unique communication between your Higher Self and your current physical being.

It may be difficult to grasp that your Higher Self at higher dimensional levels does not have the same associations with Symbols that you may have in the current lifetime, having experienced the emotional association with the Symbol in another life and not the current one. For this reason, if no present lifetime association is found, your fear (of water) may be considered irrational, and you are then said to have developed phobias based on forgotten and usually mythical experiences you had as a child in the current lifetime. Regardless of the fear's origins, however, what is clear and usually not recognized is that the Symbol has stirred a unique feeling in you, and the emotion it evokes, as well as the intensity of the feeling brought forth, is actually a unique form of communication between you and your Higher Self.

Of utmost importance to understand in this equation is that Symbols and Symbolism possess highly tuned vibrational qualities. Look around you, wherever you currently find yourself, and notice the emotion evoked by any object on which you fix your attention. If you are being truthful, every object in the room, itself a visual Symbol of some kind, will evoke memories, thoughts and feelings, and you would be hard pressed to find any single item or object that does not have some meaning or cause some emotional response in you. An object that did not do so would vanish from your sight and potentially not be perceived by you at all.

In the dream state, you experiment with what you visualize and its vibrational quality and compatibility to you, and to your life mission, before drawing a matching vibration into actual physical form as you create your reality. But it is important to understand that the exact Symbol (object) that may be pictured in your dream state is not necessarily what is made manifest in your realty. Rather, a vibrational "match" is made and what is generally made manifest in your physical reality is an object or event that has a similar vibrational quality to the Symbol in question. In essence, a vibrational parallel is created for you, by you.

It must also be understood that your reality is comprised almost entirely of Symbols that are visualized and speak to you, knowingly or not. The image or form created however is merely a matter of convenience. Whatever image a Symbol might use for its expression, it is the vibrational quality of that Symbol that holds the relevance with respect to the creation of your reality.

Returning to our example, although water holds a unique Symbolism for each viewer, everyone might consciously agree that it appears blue. It is agreed via the mass consciousness backdrop that water shall appear blue in some form to everyone. It is this agreement on the object's imagery at the mass consciousness level that allows water to be created in physical form in a format that most agree upon and see. But it is water's vibration, felt at an unconscious level through its emotional interaction with you, that speaks the language of symbolism. This is the reality of water that you do not recognize, and this is the start of a dialogue between you and your Higher Self, and your Higher Self and you.

Imagine that a song comes on the radio. It is a song about riding horses across the horizon into a glorious sunset. For many, the literal image is clear - horses riding into the sunset, nothing more, nothing less. But for some, it immediately evokes the emotion of being happy and free. For yet another individual, it evokes the emotional memory of a loved one who has passed from physical life who once was an avid lover of horses.

In real terms, the Symbol is now a direct link with that loved one for the person, and the emotional state confirms it. Whenever the image of riding horses into the sunset is present, this person is immediately connected with his or her loved one (thought is action), not only in a symbolic way but also in real terms at higher vibrational levels difficult for you to understand. That Symbol, which is quite different from its actual literal imagery, has now been transformed into an important part of the language this individual is speaking to himself (or herself) and to the deceased loved one.

The communication triggered by the Symbol has summoned the love one by way of messaging through the Higher Self. And in much the same way that loved one who has passed from your reality might have been the facilitator in bringing the image to your attention with the assistance of your Higher Self and your unconscious. So the Language of Symbols has now transcended even the boundaries of physical life and astral existence, if you are willing to understand what is actually happening. Photographs, as an example, do this all the time. Unfortunately however, you most likely relegate the feeling and emotion you feel at seeing the photo of that departed loved one as fantasy. It is not, and the momentary glance and emotion you feel is as much a two-way communication, albeit a silent one at a higher vibrational level, as any you might have that day.

But let's take this a bit further. Perhaps there is someone who hears this same song on the radio and suddenly they are faced with fits of sadness and remorse. In another lifetime, perhaps they were thrown from a horse at that very time of day and made lame for that lifetime, or even killed instantaneously. The symbol now has a very different vibrational quality and meaning. In this case, if you are being attentive to your emotional response, the different symbolism for the same imagery is now providing you with a personal gauge, light if you will, informing you of what may need healing in this lifetime, or something that is in the process of being healed within you right now.

Understanding the unique meaning behind your own Symbols then, despite the generic objects and images that comprise them, recognizing what the Symbols mean for you and especially acknowledging your feelings when faced with a Symbol, should be considered primary insight into your inner world and your Higher Self. Not only is this true in terms of the current lifetime, but it is also applicable to all lifetimes related to you and the connection you have to both your Essence Path and your Soul.

You are beginning to understand that energy creates your world. As you become accustom to this thinking, you see that primal vibrational frequencies and scalar energies, such as those inherent in light and sound, are also instrumental in manifesting reality. When light or sound is cast upon anything, the scalar vibration of particles is obliged into real form. Symbolic images, formed under the laws of dimensional physics and agreed upon by virtue of mass consciousness, is the further individualization of energy as form, and thus the Symbols and objects you create are not only part of a primary language used to communicate inter-dimensionally, they are also an integral part of the process of creation as well.

Nowhere is this more apparent than in the creation stories passed down to you where one statement stands out against the intertwined and misleading mythologies: "In the beginning was the Word." This is often misinterpreted, and we would like to suggest that you understand this statement in a new and unique way.

The "Word" is merely another way of expressing what we have described as a "Symbol", the basis of a universal language. When placed in the presence of scalar energy and combined with vibrational intent (emotion), the Word, or Symbol as the case may be, is powerful enough to trigger creation, the creation of not only your personal and world physical reality, but of the Universe and all the dimensions it contains.

The Meaning of 11:11

Q: I've been seeing a lot more 11:11, 22:22, etc., than ever before. They seem to be increasing for me personally. Is that in anticipation of the new energy coming? Is there more messaging in this?

First of all, it must be understood that everything in the Universe has a vibrational signature. It is for this reason that even your words are important, for the word when spoken is a vibrational frequency that attracts to itself creation. But more important even than this is the coding of symbolism and vibration that is inherent for the Human species. For those individuals of opening higher consciousness, the vibrational signatures that are being noticed more frequently of late are seen in what we shall call the master numbers: 11, 22, 33, 44, 55, etc.

Though not entirely precise, it is nonetheless sufficient to say that each of these master number vibrations is encoded in the human species within the DNA, and as such they have a specific meaning and significance that is registered by you in either a conscious or an unconscious way. Until now, these vibrational symbols and signatures have only been triggered in an unconscious manner. But now, due to the rising consciousness that you have, your recognition of them and the synchronicity experienced with regard to seeing them is because, as we have remarked, they are important symbols that have been coded into life, your DNA, and an awareness of that coding is emerging at this time.

Each of these master signatory vibrational symbols has meaning and while we cannot here discuss each of them, the one that you are questioning with respect to the number 11:11 has a symbolic meaning related to the opening of your consciousness. This number sequence, which has been present in your world for millennia but is only now becoming a form of gifted awareness, particularly over the course of several years, is in fact related to unlocking certain coded signals in you that are related to understanding consciously that the time of grand "opening" has come. Therefore, we would very much associate 11:11 with the coming winter solstice 2012, and the period we have described when your planetary system is entering the electromagnetic band (cloud) in space known as the photon belt. 11:11 signifies and evokes in you the understanding that the dimensional doorway has opened and you have entered a new energetic realm in both a literal and philosophical sense.

You will find shortly that other master numbers will begin to resonate and become important to you as well. In particular, you will notice the numbers 3:33 or 4:44. These have coded significance with regard to the direction of your consciousness with respect to your journey as a Soul and, particularly with respect to 4:44, your connection to the Astral Plane, your astral body and others that have passed before you and are residing in the higher astral realms at this time.

Suffice to say for now that 11:11 is significant principally in triggering in you certain vested knowledge that begins your journey on the path of opening consciousness and higher awareness related to the photon energies coming from the photon belt and the Galactic Center. We would add to this that were you to investigate, you would find that many of the legitimate crop circles that have appeared around your world at this time are also related to this symbolic signature and when seen, without conscious understanding, have the effect of triggering your desire to evolve (become aware) and opening your consciousness in various ways as well. Most crop circles utilize sacred geometric shapes formulated encoded master vibrational equations, and their symbolism is intended to inspire or trigger in you a sympathetic resonance that allows you to unlock the doors of awareness found deep inside of you. We would add that were you to examine crop circles as mathematical and geometric theorems and equations, you would find that many of them equate to the resonance of the master number 11:11 that is related to entry into this new level of consciousness – a symbol for awakening the conscious opening and new potential for growth that is being revealed at this time.

OTHER ESSENCE PATH BOOKS

"Timeline Collapse & Universal Ascension: The Future of Third Dimensional Earth and Fifth Dimensional Terra"

"What we have attempted to explain in this book is that although history carefully constructs historic conflicts and events so they can be placed within specific regions at certain time periods, seemingly without connection, the truth from a Soul and karmic perspective is that these things are far more universal, multidimensional, ongoing, interconnected, unending, ebbing and flowing than they may appear. In fact, they transpire over many hundred and even thousand-year intervals with the participation of Souls who keep coming, going and returning, again and again, for purposes related to continuing their own Soul growth and karmic balancing."

Over a decade of telepathic work has led to the astounding revelations compiled in the Essence Path series. Book Four in the Series, "Timeline Collapse & Universal Ascension: The Future of Third Dimensional Earth and Fifth Dimensional Terra" continues an extraordinary journey into higher levels of spiritual guidance and awakening. Part One provides us with new detailed information concerning the collapse and regeneration of the current Third Dimensional timeline, predictions concerning major world events as they appear on that timeline from now through the 26th Century, and an explanation of why there is an ever widening rift between those destined to continue on within Third Dimensional incarnations and those destined, through Ascension, to incarnate on a higher vibrational version of Earth called Terra. Part Two opens an unprecedented window into the Ascension of Human Angelic Souls with details of life on Fifth Dimensional Terra, including its many extraordinary features, and an analysis of galactic events seen on the future timeline of the Fifth Dimension.

a FORETHOUGHT PUBLISHING *book*

www. ESSENCE*path*.com

"The System Lords and the Twelve Dimensions: New Revelations Concerning the Dimensional Shift of 2012-2250 and the Evolution of Human Angelics"

"The 'End-Time' tales of woe and foreboding concerning 2012 that you have heard are only relevant in that they generate fear, which closes you off from the higher vibrational energies seeking to activate your DNA and cellular structure at this time. From our perspective this is far from the end, but rather a truly miraculous turning point for mankind, Earth and the entire Solar System. Your world finds itself in a state of transformation, a transition related to the collapse of your current time line and your emergence into a higher universal vibration and new dimensional reality. It is through this process, known as Ascension, that every individual Soul, Earth itself and all worlds in the universe evolve. In that regard, you are living at an extraordinary moment indeed."

This book, "The System Lords and the Twelve Dimensions: *New Revelations Concerning the Dimensional Shift of 2012-2250 and the Evolution of Human Angelics*" builds on themes began in "Discovering Your Essence Path," Book One and Book Two of the Essence Path series, providing us with a more complete analysis of coming Earth changes, the reasons an intensification of energy is coming from the Galactic core and altering our Solar System at this time, the collapse of our dimensional time line, the evolution of our DNA, the structure of the multi-dimensional universe and how the vibrational quality of our beliefs, emotions, thoughts and choices combine to raise our cellular resonance. Book Three also provides an in depth examination of Soul polarity, so-called "alien" exchanges, what to expect in the coming Golden Age and an overview of our dimension's interaction with Ninth Dimensional System Lords, Avatars who return periodically to our world and incarnate in human form to facilitate momentous leaps in consciousness like the one we are now experiencing-a time that promises to be one of the most monumental periods in the history of the planet.

a FORETHOUGHT PUBLISHING *book*

www. ESSENCE*path*.com

"Fear, Faith and Physical Reality"

"...And what's all this talk about a new age of peace, harmony and happiness? It is insight, and, in many cases, guidance related to the understanding that within the current synchronicity, where physical materialization of reality is sped-up, a world based on Faith (not the religious kind, but the kind that accepts that life's events have a purpose orchestrated and understood by your soul if not by your conscious waking self) will attract events and situations of a like kind. But a world based on your Fear will attract into it, faster than ever before, exactly what is feared. More and more, your predisposition for a lifetime wrought with endless challenge, or a life filled with peace, harmony and happiness, is directly related to whether you are aligned vibrationally with the frequency of Fear or Faith."

This book, "Fear, Faith and Physical Reality," Book Two from the "DISCOVERING YOUR ESSENCE PATH" series, builds on the themes began in Book One providing a more complete analysis of the coming vibrational changes, description of the coming emergence of 4th dimension attributes within the 3rd dimension, the nature of universal dimensional overlap, the polarity of belief, emotion and thought and your relationship to the manifestation of your personal reality. Book Two also examines further the reasons mastering Fear and maintaining Faith by understanding the purpose of your Higher Self during the lifetime is paramount to a successful life mission, and how your ability to carry light (en-"lighten"-ment) at the cellular level -- a component of the vibrational signature that identifies your Soul throughout the universe -- is being increased exponentially as we approach one of the most transforming periods in Earth's history.

Almost a decade of telepathic work communicating with a group of entities that collectively have identified themselves as "Samuel" has led to the breakthrough information compiled in the "DISCOVERING YOUR ESSENCE PATH" series. Book Two, "Fear, Faith and Physical Reality" continues your journey to higher levels of spiritual guidance through the understanding of your Essence.

a FORETHOUGHT PUBLISHING *book*

www. ESSENCE*path*.com

"Your Essence Path and Other Quintessential Phenomena"

"Life can truly be seen as a dance. It is your Higher Self that is leading this dance, holding you up as you guide across the ballroom floor. When you are in touch with and accepting of your Higher Self's lead, you enter into the flow of the dance and your life is smooth and seemingly effortless. But when you refuse the lead of your Higher Self, distracted by fear and your Ego, you stumble and fall out of sync...Continue to resist, and the pull will be so great as to knock you to the ground. In metaphysical or symbolic terms, this is the dance of life."

This book, "YOUR ESSENCE PATH AND OTHER QUINTESSENTIAL PHENOMENA," Book One from the "DISCOVERING YOUR ESSENCE PATH" series, builds the foundation for a unique understanding of the interaction between your Higher Self and your physically-bound self. ESSENCE PATH provides the knowledge and techniques you need to begin the discovery of your Essence, or Soul, path. In addition, Book One explores the nature of our causal reality and its relationship to thought, feeling and the fabric of life, the multi-dimensional nature of your Soul and its journey, the truth about higher guidance in the 3rd Dimensional realm, the world altering energetic changes we are facing and relevance those changes will have to our lives, how dreams and the astral state contribute to your reality, and the reasons why increasing your energetic vibration through higher consciousness is particularly important as we fast approach the monumental 2012 time period.

Almost a decade of telepathic work communicating with a group of entities that collectively have identified themselves as "Samuel" has led to the breakthrough information compiled in the "Discovering Your Essence Path" series. Book One, "Your Essence Path and Other Quintessential Phenomena" begins your journey to a new level of higher guidance and understanding of your Essence.

a FORETHOUGHT PUBLISHING *book*

w w w . ESSENCE*path*.com

Made in the USA
Middletown, DE
07 November 2020